POWER STORIES

POWER STORIES

The 8 stories you MUST tell to build an epic business

VALERIE **KHOO**

WILEY

John Wiley & Sons, Australia, Ltd

First published in 2013 by John Wiley & Sons Australia, Ltd

42 McDougall St, Milton Qld 4064

Office also in Melbourne

Typeset in ITC Berkeley Oldstyle Std Book 11/12

© Valerie Khoo 2013

The moral rights of the author have been asserted

National Library of Australia Cataloguing-in-Publication data:

Author:	Khoo, Valerie.
Title:	Power stories: the 8 stories you must tell to build an epic business/Valerie Khoo.
ISBN:	9781118387511 (pbk.)
Subjects:	Self-actualization (Psychology). Achievement motivation.
Dewey Number:	158.1

Cover design by Michael Cook

Cover image: © Pedro Nogueira/Veer

Back cover author photo: <www.GinaMilicia.com>

Printed in China by Printplus Limited

10 9 8 7 6 5 4 3 2 1

Disclaimer

The material in this publication is of the nature of general comment only, and does not represent professional advice. It is not intended to provide specific guidance for particular circumstances and it should not be relied on as the basis for any decision to take action or not take action on any matter which it covers. Readers should obtain professional advice where appropriate, before making any such decision. To the maximum extent permitted by law, the author and publisher disclaim all responsibility and liability to any person, arising directly or indirectly from any person taking or not taking action based on the information in this publication.

To Peter, Rex, Rocky, Rambo, Dougal and Groucho

Contents

About the author

Valerie Khoo is a journalist, keynote speaker and one of Australia's most popular small business commentators. She is also a successful entrepreneur in her own right. With a passion for both storytelling and business, Valerie founded the Sydney Writers' Centre in 2005. It is now Australia's leading centre for writing courses, with students from all over the world enrolled in its online programs.

Valerie leads a team of presenters featuring Australia's top writing trainers, journalists and authors who teach a wide range of courses in all genres of writing. The Sydney Writers' Centre was a winner in the prestigious Telstra Business Awards NSW (2010) and was named by Dell as one of the 10 most innovative small businesses in Australia (2009). You can find out more at <www.SydneyWritersCentre.com.au>.

Valerie's popular Enterprise column about entrepreneurship appears on Fairfax news sites across Australia. She is ambassador of the annual Best Australian Blogs Competition and her personal blog, <www.ValerieKhoo.com>, was named by SmartCompany as one of the 25 Best Business Blogs in Australia in 2011. Valerie is also an investor and mentor to businesses and start-ups.

Introduction

Power stories. What are they? Why do you need them? And what difference can they make in your life? Power stories are the stories you tell to influence, inspire and persuade. This book will show you how you can harness the hidden power of stories to make a difference in every part of your life. Whether you want to win a promotion at work, convince a customer to sign on the dotted line or inspire a group of people to action, the right stories can make it happen.

But what if you're not a natural storyteller or writer? What if you're never the guy at the barbecue who has everyone cracking up at your jokes or tall tales? What if you're never the one with the riveting stories to tell of your girls' night out? What if you simply don't think you have any interesting stories to tell?

This book shows you easy ways to identify the stories that will help you get what you want and reveals the simple techniques that can turn you into a master storyteller. You'll discover how you can use stories to transform your business, create opportunities and, in some cases, maybe even change the world.

So why storytelling? These days, storytelling is one of the most underrated and underused tools that we use in life. But this wasn't always the case. In ancient times, stories were the primary mode of communication. Stories were told through carvings and cave paintings; they were shared around the campfire and at tribal gatherings, and passed on from generation to generation. Stories explained the world around us and helped us make sense of it.

Now, in our hyper-connected online world, our connections are often reduced to 140-character tweets, pithy status updates about what we're doing, and one-click declarations on Facebook about what we 'like'. We are less likely to take the time to share compelling stories when it's so much easier simply to blurt out an opinion on Twitter, whether it's about a TV show or the lousy service at a fancy restaurant.

These instant interactions have their place—and they *do* make us feel connected—but storytelling is often lost in the process. It's time to bring back the art—and power—of storytelling into our lives. It's vital to bring it back into the way we do business. Storytelling is intrinsic to the human experience because we're hardwired to understand and tell stories.

For most of us, participating in storytelling—either passively as a listener or actively as the teller—is the most natural thing in the world. We're all born with the storytelling gene. In some of us it's been suppressed but, like an unused muscle, it's still there. And once you start to exercise it, this muscle will become stronger and more powerful.

It may be lying under years of fat—that is, the conditioning we go through in the corporate world, where statistics, spreadsheets and pie charts have come to rule our communications. It may never have been awoken, if you grew up in a family that simply didn't communicate through stories. It may be hidden under the surface static of social media activity, photo tagging and blog commenting. Beneath this online chatter about last night's reality show winners are the real stories in your life that *should* be told. Once you strip back today's social conditioning, you'll find your natural instinct for storytelling.

It's an instinct you can use to your advantage. You can use stories to inspire and lead your team. You can use them to persuade customers to buy or venture capitalists to invest. In a world of email blasts and 30-second, attention-grabbing advertising blitzes, you can use the subtler power of stories to convert customers and build a legion of fans.

You can use stories to make yourself stand out in a crowd and be remembered. Stories can help you build your personal brand and boost your profile. Remember that stories aren't just about people. They can be about ideas, causes and products too. You just need to work out the best way to tell your stories to achieve your goals.

Sometimes we shy away from personal storytelling because we perceive our lives as pretty, well, ordinary. If life seems like a continuous loop of feeding kids, cleaning up, driving them to sport, picking them up and feeding them again, you may feel like the only stories you have to tell are about vomit, tantrums and sleep deprivation. Similarly, if life has slipped into the routine of a long commute to the office, where every day is predictably the same, and if you fundamentally don't believe that you have any interesting stories of your own, it can feel safer to dwell on inconsequential stories about Lindsay Lohan's latest courtroom appearance or some juicy Hollywood gossip.

What's happened to *your* stories?

In this book, you'll discover the key power stories you need to get ahead, build your profile and grow your business. It's not difficult, because you are tapping into a fundamental human skill that's already inside you.

In chapter 1, you'll discover how storytelling has evolved, why it's so important to use it in your business, and how you can use it to convince stakeholders, inspire followers and convert customers. Then, buckle up, as we're going for a ride in chapter 2 — on the Entrepreneur's Journey. You'll identify how this journey will underpin your power stories.

In chapter 3, you'll identify your passion story and determine how you can use this to intrigue the people you meet. Your business story in chapter 4 will be the core focus on your website and in many of your marketing materials. It's vital to get this right. In chapter 5, you'll discover one of the most powerful stories of all — your customer story. You'll learn how to collect, identify and use these stories to their best effect.

If you're starting out in business, or if you have an innovative concept to share, you'll learn how to craft your pitch story in chapter 6. Selling products can be a challenge, but learning how to develop a strong product story in chapter 7 will get you halfway there.

Like it or not, as an entrepreneur you're a leader. You lead staff, customers and maybe even a legion of raving fans. In chapter 8, you'll learn how your leader's story can inspire people and maybe even change the world. In chapter 9, you'll discover how the right media story will create headlines about your business and build your media profile.

After creating an arsenal of stories, you then need to share them. But what makes a story catch on? What motivates other people to share your stories—and effectively do your marketing for you? You'll find out in chapter 10. Finally, in chapter 11, you'll discover ... the most important story of all.

This is the sort of book you can simply read and enjoy, taking away the ideas that most resonate for you. Or you can use it as a workbook, ensuring that you have identified your eight stories by the time you have finished. If that's your purpose, I've provided you with an exclusive resource of tools and templates at <www.powerstoriesbook.com>, only available to readers of this book.

If you're ready to unlock the storyteller inside you, be prepared for the magic that's about to unfold. Be ready to tell your story.

CHAPTER 1

It's all about connection

When I was growing up, I used to catch the train to Sutherland Library in the southern suburbs of Sydney after school, where I'd wait for my father to pick me up when he finished work. I used to love hanging out at the library. I wish I could tell you I spent my time reading the encyclopedia because I wanted to be a rocket scientist or devouring literary classics so I could become a great writer. But that would be stretching the truth — in fact, it would be nowhere near it. My love for the library was not so ... intellectual.

As soon as I set foot in the library each day I would head over to the magazine section, where well-thumbed copies of teen magazines were in abundant supply. I'm talking about the magazines for girls who were obsessed with celebrities, boys, fashion, boys, makeup, boys, TV stars, being cool at school and, oh, did I mention boys? I was in heaven.

My parents were very proud because they thought their daughter was studying hard enough to get into Mensa. In reality, I was becoming an expert on the *really important things* in life, like what Jon Bon Jovi liked to eat for breakfast, how to get rid of blackheads, and when it was okay to wear legwarmers. (Note: I learned much later in life that the answer to the last was 'Never'.)

It wasn't just about the celebrities, beauty and fashion. I also loved reading the articles about real people. At the time, the teen magazines featured inspirational stories about young women who were making it big in sport, music or some other chosen field, or who were on the road to recovery after struggling with an eating disorder. And, of course, there was the obligatory story about the girl-next-door who was spotted in a shopping mall by a talent scout who set her on the path to becoming an international supermodel.

When I wasn't wondering when this was going to happen to me (in case you're interested, that talent scout never did tap me on the shoulder), it was the magazine stories about other readers that had me most riveted. Because they were about other people, just like me, these stories played a huge part in helping me make sense of the world around me.

Look, I don't pretend this is where I came to understand the intricacies about the conflict in the Middle East or how the International Monetary Fund's decisions affected the global economy during the '80s. But it's where I discovered how other people saw the world and how they dealt with their problems. It made me wonder what I would do in a similar situation. It was through these real stories that I learned about friendship, sexuality, dating, nutrition and much more. It was also through stories about real people that I learned about different career choices beyond accounting, law or medicine — the only three careers that ever seemed to be discussed in our household.

As an only child, I didn't have any brothers or sisters to compare notes with. And while I had loving parents, we weren't the sort of family that had big conversations about issues or emotions. We were more likely to be watching *The Price Is Right* during dinner than debating politics or telling stories.

As I grew up, my reading transitioned from teen magazines to everything from *Vanity Fair* and *The New Yorker* to Australia's *Good Weekend*. While some of my girlfriends would pore over fashion magazines, coveting the latest handbag from Gucci or Hermès,

I would get lost in the feature articles. I loved nothing more than letting the writers take me on a journey into someone else's world, where I would learn about their joys, pains, struggles or quirks. Two thousand words later, I felt just that little bit richer through knowing their story.

This is where I developed my love for the written word and my love for stories. I know it would be far more romantic and dramatic to say that it was Shakespeare, George Orwell or J.D. Salinger who ignited this passion. But the truth is it was the glossy pages of these magazines that nurtured my love of reading and writing through real stories about real people.

Don't get me wrong. I loved to be absorbed in a novel or movie. I used to be in awe of the imagination of the writers who could create believable alternative worlds like Tolkien's Middle Earth or Isaac Asimov's spellbinding future visions, or larger-than-life characters like F. Scott Fitzgerald's Gatsby. Some of these stories moved me to the core. Yes, I cried while reading the last few pages of *Hamlet*, and I was determined to fight prejudice after reading *To Kill a Mockingbird*, but I was also inspired to take up boxing thanks to the tales of Rocky Balboa. These stories—in books or movies—were all created from someone's imagination, and they were no less powerful than real ones.

But there was something about real stories that just resonated with me. If they could happen to other people, they could happen to me. So I found them endlessly fascinating. It's no surprise that I eventually became a writer and journalist. I loved unearthing these stories: discovering the passions, struggles, setbacks and triumphs in other people's lives—and I loved to write about them in a way that could inspire others, or at least help them make sense of what may have been going on in their own lives.

The part that excites me is not the act of putting words on a page. It's not about getting the structure of a sentence right, or ensuring the right adjectives or nouns are used in the narrative. Those are just some of the technical steps to achieving the ultimate goal, which is fundamentally about connection. Connecting with another person. Your aim might to be inform, entertain, inspire, educate or motivate. But, ultimately, it's about connecting with another human being—simply by telling a story.

Once upon a time...

Stories are a fundamental part of human existence. They've been around since the beginning of time. Long before there were newspapers, water coolers, books or blogs, stories were simply shared around the campfire, at tribal gatherings or through pictures on cave walls.

Sharing stories is one of the most natural human instincts we possess, and it's fundamental to the way we communicate. Throughout the ages, humans have used stories to explain phenomena, convey information, record history and make sense of our own and others' behaviour.

Cavemen used pictures to tell hunting stories. Before writing evolved as a tool to record and communicate, storytelling was the only way we preserved history and ensured our rituals and practices continued through generations. Egyptians told stories through hieroglyphs carved on walls or written on papyrus. Sometimes these stories recorded facts, but not always.

People have always told stories to explained the unexplainable. That distant rumbling in the skies that eventually turned into an 'oh we're going to die' boom overhead? Long before our ancient forebears rationalised the concept of thunder, they created stories about the god of thunder. And those yellow and orange flames that flickered into life when we rubbed two sticks together? Well, they too were explained by a mythical deity that could create fire. Superstitions, traditions and rituals often have their origins in stories.

Stories stand the test of time. The Greek poet Homer is thought to have composed the *Iliad* and the *Odyssey* around the 8th century BC, and these great epics are still studied today. Great storytellers such as Moses, Jesus, Mohammed and Buddha garnered both followers and fanatics as a result of their stories. Religious movements and philosophies have spread all over the world through the telling and retelling of their stories. Whether they are about the search for redemption or salvation, or sitting under a tree waiting for enlightenment, these stories work because in some way they connect with something inside us.

With the advent of the printing press, stories were no longer shared among small groups of people. Finally, these stories could be spread from one to many. The fairytales of the Brothers Grimm and Hans Christian Andersen are known to children around the world, illustrating how powerful stories can be. They can be used to inspire or scare, to motivate or manipulate, to empower or dominate.

Throughout history people have embraced the power of storytelling, for good or ill. Adolf Hitler's rise to power can be partly attributed to his story, as told in his autobiography and political manifesto, *Mein Kampf* ('My Struggle'). Hitler knew how to use stories to his advantage, but he also encouraged book-burning campaigns to destroy the stories that ran counter to his own. China's Mao Zedong used stories both to galvanise, and eventually devastate, a nation. *The Little Red Book*, a selection of quotations from his speeches and writings, helped communicate the ideology of China's Communist Party. Britain's Winston Churchill, through his rallying speeches, used stories to bring hope and inspiration to a country facing the depths of war.

In today's digital world, companies and brands convey their stories in 30-second bites. Blogs, social media and other online sharing platforms have broadened the one-to-many model into potentially one-to-millions.

Why is storytelling so powerful?

A story is so simple. But sometimes the simplest things can have the greatest impact. Throughout history we've seen the power of storytelling in action, but exactly what part of the storytelling process inspires or moves people? It's when we explore this question that we discover why stories reach our very core.

Stories can make or break whether you score a deal with a new client. They can be decisive in convincing a jury to convict someone or to set them free. They're powerful because they package data, logic and analysis into an easily digestible form — easy to tell, easy to remember, easy to understand and, ultimately, easy to share.

Let's say I'm looking after your cat while you're on holidays. If you tell me to give your cat some flea treatment, I'll understand your instruction intellectually. I may even remember to do it. But if you package that in a story about how you forgot to give your last cat his flea treatment, and he got a tick and went into a coma, I'll remember that, and I'm much more likely to make sure he gets his treatment! An instruction is much more powerful when there's a story attached to it.

Our brains absorb and retain stories more readily than lists of numbers or reams of data. A story packages an impersonal, forgettable series of facts and figures in a format that we can connect with, and that can be easily shared. It's hard to get people excited about lists or bullet points. But tell them a story and they're more likely to pay attention. They're also more likely to pass it on.

A story's strength also lies in its subtlety. Stories may be anecdotes, commentary, opinions. They may be chronicles of people, ideas and places. Yet their power can be far-reaching, even subversive. When you tell a story, you invite listeners or readers to draw their own conclusions. But tell your story well and you can shape what those conclusions will be. Good stories are powerful because they are not oppressive or didactic. Rather, they motivate or inspire others to feel and act of their own accord.

A story is much greater than the sum of its parts. It has information and ideas embedded within it, perhaps with facts, figures, dialogue and characters. Put together, they are no longer a collection of disparate elements. They can create a whole that has its own force, momentum and influence.

So what's happened to the art of storytelling recently? There's still a strong storytelling culture in the arts. Movies are as popular as ever. Books are still in demand, albeit the medium for reading is shifting towards a more digital experience.

But in the world of business and the workplace, it's a different story…

The decline of storytelling

Picture this. You're watching someone do a presentation at work. Or maybe you're in an audience of your peers at an industry conference. The presenter heads up to the lectern, introduces himself then starts his PowerPoint presentation. Now this scenario generally plays out in one of two ways. In one scenario, the presenter is a good storyteller who knows how to use a slide presentation as a useful tool to enhance his story.

Please God, make it so.

In the other more common scenario, though, the presenter's innate storytelling skills have been steamrolled by years of corporate conditioning, which means he's been brainwashed into thinking that statistics, data, graphs and pie charts will engage and convince his audience.

Oh no, another Death by PowerPoint. How long is it till lunch?

Chances are you've experienced something like this. Your colleague or boss—who usually has no problem amusing you with stories at the company picnic or at Friday night drinks—turns into an autobot who seems capable only of reading directly from the PowerPoint slide.

Word. For. Freaking. Word.

And we're not talking about just a few succinct, telling words here. He appears to have copied massive chunks of text into the slide and inserted a few random bullet points because, well, that's what you do when you create a slide presentation, isn't it? He even says: 'I know you can read this yourself later but I thought it would be useful to put this on a slide for you …'

The man's a genius.

This is invariably accompanied by an announcement that the slides will be available on Slideshare or can be emailed to all participants so you don't need to bother taking down notes from the mini-novel that has appeared on the screen.

Because I'm just SO engaged in this presentation that I can't wait to download the slides and relive the experience in my own time later.

Then this presenting genius, who may actually have a valid and wonderful story to tell underneath this slideshow, projects a series of graphs on the screen. After all, he just spent hours working in Excel to turn his raw data into a fancy line graph with different colours representing various cost centres within the company extrapolated over a five-year period. To top it off, he's overlaid a bar chart to compare these figures with industry benchmarks.

I think I need glasses. Is it just me? Can anyone else see what's on the screen?

The presenter explains: 'I know you won't be able to see the detail in this graph from where you are …'

Why in the world did you include a slide we can't … um … SEE?

And with a click of the remote he moves on to the next slide: 'I know you can't see this next slide either, but I thought I'd include it anyway …'

What the …? Okay, that's it. I'm going to tweet a photo of the slide so everyone can see how ridiculous this looks.

At this point he includes a mindmap that's supposed to offer an overview of the industry. It's impossibly complex, and uses a 6-point font that would require bionic vision to read, so you're simultaneously going cross-eyed and feeling nauseated trying to make sense of it.

I wonder if anyone would notice if I snuck out of this presentation right now?

He reels off more statistics, presents a few industry averages (accompanied with some cheesy clipart) and makes a statement (which you forget instantly) about why it's so important to embrace this strategy. He then wraps up with a closing slide encouraging the audience to connect with him on LinkedIn or Twitter.

So you can then bore me witless in 140 characters? I don't think so.

Where's the story? Where's the passion? What, in this sea of text and graphs, was supposed to connect with his audience?

It's not fair to blame this all on PowerPoint. In fact, PowerPoint can actually be a powerful tool to help you tell stories. But too often it's used as a crutch in order to *avoid* telling stories. This is because of the conventions we've been subjected to, particularly in the business world. We've been told that data is king. That we can't make any useful business decisions unless we have the data to support us. And lots of it.

The number crunchers who have to sign off on strategic business decisions want to see it in black or white—specifically in spreadsheets that can be manipulated, data-mined and turned into those all-important pretty graphs. They are the ones who chant: 'The numbers speak for themselves', when in reality the numbers tell only half the story.

They may believe that data and numerical evidence should have the final say. When it comes to influencing people, data might be king, but the ace up your sleeve is your story. Use the right data in a good *story*, and you have a powerful combination that can influence behaviour and, sometimes, change the world.

Data can convince the mind, but you need a story framing that data so that you can reach people's emotions and make them truly believe in what you have to say. It's not just the pathetic PowerPoint presenters that are killing storytelling in the workplace in favour of clinical numbers. In recent years, the explosion in online communication has also taken a toll on our storytelling abilities.

Remember when we used to go into stores and talk to sales assistants? You know, actual humans. Before eBay, Amazon and online shopping we used to talk to people in real life. Whether it was conscious or instinctive, they would tell us stories about the products or the difference the products or services made in the lives of other customers. And these stories shaped our decisions on whether or not to buy. Now, we have online shopping carts that list exciting information like:

Zamatek E350
1.6 GHz; AMD Brazos platform
2 GB 1333 MHz DDR3; 2 SODIMM
320 GB SATA (7200 rpm)
SuperMulti SATA drive and double layer supporting Everlight Technology
ATI Odeon HD 6310 (up to 256 MB)
20" integrated TFT panel
8 USB 2.0; 6-in-1 memory card reader
USB optical wired mouse; USB keyboard
Integrated 10/100 BaseT network interface (broadband ready)
HP wireless NIC 802.11b/g/n mini card

If you're a techie or a geek, this might actually mean something to you. But to the rest of us mortals, this is not what we would call riveting, or even useful, reading.

Short but not so sweet

Not only have we been conditioned to embrace this emphasis on numbers, data and quantifiable information in our working lives, but we've also become attuned to shorter communications, with abbreviated language and emoticons replacing meaningful exchanges.

OMG. LOL. ROFL. *(Oh my God. Laugh out loud. Rolling on the floor laughing.)*
Kthxbai *(Okay thanks goodbye.)*
Thx. IMHO u r awesome. GTG. KIT. *(Thanks. In my humble opinion you are awesome. Got to go. Keep in touch.)*

Okay, maybe you don't use these abbreviations too often. But look at the posts of any number of the 200 million Twitter users—or the chat history of any teenager and you'll see that this form of communication is the norm. Twitter limits your messages to 140 characters. When I'm trying to condense a long message so I can tweet it, I sometimes find myself sounding like an inarticulate idiot with the vocabulary of a preschooler. But this is the way many people are staying in contact.

Yesteryear's campfire gathering is today's Twitter stream or Facebook status updates. Real stories are diminished in these exchanges in favour of staccato pronouncements such as 'This is my favourite place for coffee' or 'Stop live animal export NOW!'

Comments on Facebook, which now has some 900 million users, don't reassure either. These typically fall into one of the following categories:

1 'OMG sooooo cuuuute!' Or a variation thereof, usually in response to a video of a kitten falling asleep or a Labrador puppy playing with toilet paper.
2 'Want!' See point 1.
3 'That looks yum! Enjoy.' A common response to a photo of a meal about to be consumed, regardless of whether it depicts carrot sticks or caramel cheesecake.
4 'That's awesome!' Typical response to almost any announcement, ranging from a new job to a new spouse—and everything in between.
5 'Yeah, that exactly what happens with my husband/girlfriend/son/ teacher/boss/pet.' The kind of response you get when you post anything bemoaning the behaviour of any of the above.

Of course, these examples are by no means exhaustive, but they are an indication of the short, superficial nature of our communications these days. Our abbreviated communication styles have been exacerbated by the explosion of email in our inboxes. When email first came along, we responded to every one. We read every email we received and we felt that all the communication in our inbox was direct, personal, important.

Of course, this was long before we realised that all emails were not actually created equal. Alongside the emails from our friends and family were the emails from organisations trying to flog their products. Maybe you once entered a competition to win an iPad or signed up for a free ebook (and in the process provided your contact details), or you 'liked' what looked like a fun group on Facebook (and gave them permission to message you).

In the old days, businesses had to think long and hard before embarking on a marketing campaign. It was a big investment to print newsletters, catalogues and brochures and then send them through the mail. But with the advent of email, marketers can email thousands—or hundreds of thousands—of people with the simple click of a mouse.

So email marketing was born. We suddenly acquired 'friends' touting everything from Viagra to Acai berries to timeshares in exotic destinations. And we've been fighting overflowing inboxes ever since.

The attention span of goldfish

We soon became immune to this explosion in emails, however. With a finger poised over the delete key, we scan the source or subject to see if the message's fate lies in the recycle bin or if it's worth our reading time.

Marketers now know they have a slim window through which they can capture our attention. So they've ditched long stories in favour of a short paragraph about their product or service because that's all the attention they expect from you. These marketers also have webmasters and graphic designers breathing down their necks, chiding them for writing anything that will end up 'below the fold' (that is, off the screen).

Experts tell us to keep our blog posts short because our audiences have the attention span of goldfish. So we need to get to the point. Not that there's anything wrong with getting to the point, but there's a time for brevity and there's a time for story.

Please note, however, the two are not mutually exclusive. You can tell powerful stories in a limited number of words, but most of us haven't honed this skill yet. Because in the past we never had to condense our lives into such short messages. So don't get me wrong. I don't think short messages are evil. In fact, some of the most powerful stories ever told have been short. When challenged to tell a story in only six words, Ernest Hemingway came up with:

For sale: baby shoes, never worn.

Of course, most of us mere mortals don't have Hemingway's master storytelling skills. So with the rise in emails and other methods of online communication, businesses have largely ditched the art of storytelling in favour of short, sharp marketing pitches to an increasingly jaded audience. It's like the difference between a long, romantic evening of passion and a brief encounter that ends prematurely. Oops, it's over before you know it.

The evolution of journalism

Another nail in the storytelling coffin, or at least a dampener on our culture of storytelling, has been the decline of long-form or investigative journalism.

Twenty years ago I remember savouring 3000-word magazine articles every weekend. Whether a feature on an Oscar winner in *Vanity Fair* or the story of a successful entrepreneur in *Forbes*, I relished reading these stories. I would set aside time, in the bath or with a glass of wine, to let the story wash over me. These weren't pithy tales that I could read while standing on a crowded train or during TV commercial breaks. They weren't the bite-sized stories we're now served about the latest chapter in the life of a Kardashian.

The reality is that budget cuts in magazines and newspapers all over the world have resulted in shorter stories and diminished word counts. At the same time, magazines are replacing text with pictures. After all, what's more engaging to a reader: a bunch of words describing Lady Gaga giving the bird to her fans, or the actual image of her doing it, complete with a wacky outfit and sneer of contempt?

It's the message not the medium

The great thing about the art of storytelling is that it's platform neutral. Whether you are telling stories in print, movies, online or in a speech or conversation, the power lies not in the medium but *in the message*. This book focuses on the message. It will help you identify and shape the eight power stories you need to tell to grow your business. Once you're clear on what they are, they will give you a valuable arsenal you can reach into whenever you need.

You might call on a gentle story to inspire a team member into action, or a persuasive story to encourage a customer to buy, or a memorable story to help you make headlines. This book will help you nail those stories.

In this book, I talk a lot about how entrepreneurs can use storytelling to grow their business. By entrepreneur I mean anyone who is a business owner, but I am also addressing anyone in charge of running a business. You might even be an *intrapreneur*—someone who drives change and innovation within a discrete business unit in your company. If that's the case, you too can use these tools. So feel free to substitute 'entrepreneur' with whatever term you feel best fits your own role. In this book you'll find examples of how other entrepreneurs use their stories from which you can learn to adapt your own.

The way you share your stories is totally up to you. I'm not about to dictate the medium you choose for your message. While some entrepreneurs love blogging, others prefer giving keynote speeches, and yet others are addicted to Facebook. You should choose the medium that suits you—and the people you want to reach.

So what exactly are we talking about when we refer to stories in a business context anyway? Do we have to pull someone aside so we have their undivided attention before we launch into our tale? Of course not. Storytelling has come a long way since the days when you had to gather your tribe around the campfire to enchant them with the tales of your latest adventures. You don't need the captivating storytelling skills (and guitar) of Maria from *The Sound of Music* in order to settle your listeners so you can start your story from the very beginning …

Sure, storytelling in movies relies more on images, and a mesmerising speaker can make or break a speech. But both are, fundamentally, about the power of storytelling.

These days you can tell your stories through a wide variety of mediums, from a candid post on your blog to a one-on-one conversation. This can also include print brochures, YouTube videos, press articles, keynote speeches and, yes, Facebook statuses or tweets; or it may take the form of a much bigger story, encapsulated in your very own book.

In that case, what exactly is a story?
Well, if I was going to get all academic on you, I could bore you with multiple definitions of what 'experts' believe constitutes a story.

I could set out the subtle differences between these definitions and spend all day detailing the merits of each. But let's be serious, your eyes would glaze over. While the various definitions of 'story' may be important for those studying narrative structure and plot, there's no need to overcomplicate an otherwise simple concept. Let's leave that to the academics. You're an entrepreneur. You're busy! You want to get to the juicy stuff—that is, how to use your stories to grow your business.

When we talk about a story, we mean a true or fictional account of an event or events. Simple.

Throughout this book, you'll find stories as short as a sentence or paragraph, and you'll find others that go for pages. There's no hard and fast rule about how long your stories should be. But if you want them to be effective, they better be interesting and relevant to your audience.

The more your stories resonate with your audience, the more likely they will be remembered or shared. And, ultimately, isn't that what you want? When you find that other people are sharing and passing on your stories, that's when you're truly harnessing the power of storytelling to grow your business.

In the digital world there's no doubt that technology has affected the way we tell stories and communicate. The trouble is that in many cases today's technology has unwittingly dulled our storytelling skills. It's time to get them back. It's time to bring back the art—and power—of storytelling. Why? Because it can help you boost your business, increase your revenue and build a community of enthusiastic fans or customers.

If you don't think you're a natural storyteller, don't worry. The great news is that you don't need to study for four years to master the art of storytelling. Your storytelling gene is inside you waiting to be awoken. You were born with it. We all were.

You can use simple stories to grow your business, build your profile and get ahead of the pack. In the following chapters, you'll discover the eight power stories that you need to do this.

Are you ready to harness the power of storytelling?

CHAPTER 2

The entrepreneur's journey

As an entrepreneur, you're on a journey that's going to underpin most of the power stories you need to tell in order to grow your business. It's this journey—with its twists, turns, failures and successes—that will intrigue those around you, engage them with what you're doing and inspire them into action.

That's why reality shows like *The Amazing Race*, competitions like *The Apprentice* and talent programs like *The Voice* keep viewers coming back again and again. Whether or not you watch these shows, rest assured that millions of people around the world do. These shows work because they follow a pattern that's deeply ingrained in the human psyche: the Hero's Journey.

In reality shows, each viewer chooses their own hero—the competitor they want to win—and they come back week after week to travel with them on their journey. This is a fundamental principle of storytelling. It's also why readers all over the world engage with the protagonist in a story. The protagonist is the main character and, in most cases, it's this character who drives the story forward.

Through conflict, challenges and struggles, the protagonist presses on. This applies as much to James Bond's multiple missions to save the world from certain destruction as to Elizabeth Bennet's quest for romantic freedom in Jane Austen's *Pride and Prejudice* or to Rocky Balboa's journey from underdog small-time boxer to heavyweight champion of the world.

Audiences could never get enough of Rocky's trials and triumphs. Actor and writer Sylvester Stallone, the creator of the Rocky franchise, kept audiences engaged through six movies over a 30-year period. Each time, they were seized anew by Rocky's passion to win. But the essential element that makes Rocky's story, or any story, so captivating is not just the desire to win or to reach a goal. What keeps people engaged is their desire to see how the protagonist overcomes the obstacles put in his or her way.

In addition to his physical journey—the punishing training sessions and brutal fights Rocky endures—viewers are also drawn into his internal struggle. There is a deeper level of connection than simply cheering someone on to win a boxing match. In *Rocky 1* it was about proving he had what it takes to be good enough—in boxing, in love, in life. By *Rocky 6* it was about coming to terms with life after his wife's death and repairing his relationship with his son. Yes, I'm a fan. Can you tell?

Ultimately, a story is compelling when it makes an emotional connection with a reader, viewer or listener. It's safe to say that many Rocky viewers don't actually have any interest in the sport of boxing. But they relate to his passion, and they want him to overcome the odds, and to cheer him on in both his internal and his external quests.

You are the hero in your story

The Hero's Journey is a term coined by American mythologist, writer and lecturer Joseph Campbell. He describes this as the typical pattern of countless stories ranging from Jason and the Argonauts' quest for the Golden Fleece to Luke Skywalker's journey in *Star Wars*. In his book *The Hero with a Thousand Faces*, Joseph Campbell writes about how the same story is told in infinite versions, across different time periods, circumstances and cultures. It's a pattern we see played out in movies and written in books all the time.

Campbell identifies 12 steps in the Hero's Journey, but they can be summarised as:

(A) You are called to adventure (or to pursue a passion).
(B) You meet multiple obstacles and challenges along the way.
(C) You find what you are looking for.
(D) Despite this, you face more ordeals.
(E) Then you return from adventure either transformed or equipped with new knowledge or insight into the world.

Story boffins who want a more comprehensive dissection of Campbell's Hero's Journey can find the full 12 steps in the exclusive resources section at <www.powerstoriesbook.com>.

Remember, you don't have to be Luke Skywalker or an ancient Greek mythical hero to undergo this kind of journey. As an entrepreneur, you're already on a unique path that has all the elements to captivate the people around you, keep them on the edge of their seats and draw them in to support what you're doing. You're on the Entrepreneur's Journey.

In fact, the entrepreneur's journey is so closely aligned with the Hero's Journey they are practically one and the same. Let's take a look at table 2.1.

Table 2.1: the Hero's Journey and the Entrepreneur's Journey

Hero's Journey	Entrepreneur's Journey
(A) You are called to adventure.	There's that spark that nudges you to start your business.
(B) You meet multiple obstacles and challenges along the way.	Entrepreneurship is never smooth sailing. You're constantly problem-solving: there's tax, staff, building up your customer base, keeping the right inventory and so on.
(C) You find what you are looking for.	It takes time, but eventually you feel you've nailed your systems and can rely on a healthy cash flow. You've done it. Your business works!

(continued)

Table 2.1: the Hero's Journey and the Entrepreneur's Journey (*cont'd*)

Hero's Journey	Entrepreneur's Journey
(D) You face more ordeals.	But you then face a whole new set of problems. You've gone from dealing with the kinds of issues facing start-ups to the challenges that face a growing business. Maybe your key supplier goes bankrupt; your customers don't pay their bills; or you don't have enough stock to keep up with demand.
(E) You return from adventure with new knowledge and insight into the world.	Despite this, you learn, consolidate and press on. You're wiser from the experience and better equipped for the next chapter in your journey—to take your business to the next level.
The sequel.	Of course, life as an entrepreneur continues and, like the Hero's Journey, there's always room for the next adventure …

Identify your entrepreneur's journey

Have you ever taken the time to map out your entrepreneur's journey, to reflect on the key elements that make up your story? The trouble is, most people have never got around to doing this, and therein lies the problem. Just because you've lived your story doesn't mean you're any good at communicating it. You might think it should be easy to talk about your own life, passions or business, right? Well, let me assure you, this is often *not* the case. As a business journalist, I've interviewed countless entrepreneurs and many have no idea how to tell their story effectively.

Sure, a handful of them have their stories down pat, but many don't. They don't even remember the important facts, like the year they founded their business or employed their first staff member. They ramble. They remember bits and pieces of their story, and I eventually have to piece it all together like a jigsaw. This may be okay if you're talking to a journalist who has the skills to whip it into shape. But when you're talking to potential customers, suppliers or associates, you need them to concentrate on your message, rather than be busy using their brainpower to piece together your story jigsaw.

Action: write it down

Take the time right now to write down your entrepreneur's journey. It might take you half an hour, but trust me, that's time well spent. Use the categories in table 2.1 and write as much as you like. To make it even easier for you, download the template in the exclusive resources section at <www.powerstoriesbook.com>.

Grab a cup of coffee or glass of wine and think through the key steps you've taken on your journey so far. It doesn't matter if you've been in business 10 weeks or 10 years. Don't write dot points. Fill in each section as if you're telling the story to someone, as if you're having a conversation. You might take half an hour. You might take half a day.

I've worked with entrepreneurs who have found this process straightforward, simple—and a neat way to articulate their journey. I've worked with others who found in the process a cathartic release: they've finally given structure to a story that's been a disorganised mess in their brains for a long time. Whatever result you experience, I encourage you to do it, and once you've written it down, go back over it. Tweak it. Refine it. Edit it. Until it is clear, succinct and easy to share.

Once you are clear about your own story, you're going to find it a hell of a lot easier to convey it succinctly to someone else. If you hope for publicity or media coverage at some point, I strongly encourage you to go through this process so you have a strong, structured story to convey to journalists. You'll be able to draw on the right part of your story when you think it's the right 'fit' in your conversation. The core of the entrepreneur's journey is the framework on which your eight power stories will be built.

You don't have a billion-dollar business? Perhaps you wonder whether you have a business life that's interesting enough to document in the entrepreneur's journey. Well, rest assured that you don't have to be Richard Branson or Donald Trump to make the most out of this exercise. You can have a pretty normal life. Like mine.

Here are the key steps in my entrepreneur's journey so far.

(A) My call to action

After carving out a career as a journalist and editor working for newspapers and magazines, I knew it was time for a new adventure — this time, to start a business. I also knew that whatever business I started had to be deeply aligned with my passions. After all, it's passion that drives you into the wee hours when you are bootstrapping your business. It's passion that keeps you moving forward despite the obstacles and setbacks when cash flow is tight and the light appears to be getting dimmer at the end of a seemingly endless tunnel.

It's passion that underpins your entrepreneur's journey.

In my circle of friends, I've always been the Chief Cheerleader, willing my mates on to pursue their big dreams. In reality, they probably felt I was more like Chief Nagger, bugging them to achieve their goals. I have no doubt some of them got sick of my constant 'encouragement'. I knew I had to channel these energies somewhere else, as my friends probably didn't always appreciate the life coaching sessions I was giving them, regardless of the fact that they were free — and frequent.

But I was also realistic. Despite wanting to help people achieve their dreams, whatever they might be, I knew that it was unlikely I would coach anyone to Olympic gold. And I wouldn't be in a position to mentor someone to climb Everest any time soon.

There was something I knew I could definitely do, though. Combining my technical skill in writing and my passion for helping people achieve their dreams, I was in the perfect position to help people achieve their writing goals and aspirations. I knew I wanted to create a dynamic writers' centre that would become the best in Australia.

(B) Obstacles and challenges

This goal sounded very noble and exciting, but in reality I had no idea how in the world I was to make it happen. I mean, I knew how to write. I had no doubt about that. But being skilled in writing doesn't mean you know how to create, build and grow a *business* in writing.

So I had to learn. Fast.

When I first started the Sydney Writers' Centre in 2005, I was the only teacher. I was also receptionist, accountant, chief cook and bottle-washer. I did everything. Not only did I teach the first lot of classes, I was also the one who would stock the tea and coffee, buy the toilet paper and answer every single query that came over the phone or email. Needless to say, it was exhausting.

I also had to get up to speed on ever-changing tax laws, insurance, cash flows, budgets and customer relationship management systems, and learn how to direct traffic to my the website. But as enrolments kept increasing, I knew I was filling a gap in the market. Soon I employed teachers, staff and — most exciting of all — I didn't have to buy the toilet paper anymore.

(C) Finding the prize

I knew I'd hit a milestone when I went away for three weeks and the business continued to run without me. It didn't fall apart. I was stunned. The systems I had worked so hard to put in place actually worked.

Even more exciting was when we'd receive phone calls and emails from former students who wanted to tell us about the changes they had made in their lives since learning with us. Some had changed careers, others had got published in their favourite magazines, while others had signed four-book deals and had their books translated into several languages. Corporations would contact us to book hundreds of people into our courses and send their new recruits to learn the fundamentals of business writing.

Famous authors from all over the world visited the Centre. These included business gurus ranging from Robert Kiyosaki to Tim Ferriss, so I pumped them for business advice and learned about the strategies behind their best-selling books. I had to pinch myself when I realised the Centre had actually become everything I had hoped.

(D) Facing more ordeals

When your business grows, so does the number, and variety, of problems. Operational systems, IT, infrastructure, recruiting staff, suppliers that don't deliver — and finding the time to deal with them all.

After a while it seemed like Groundhog Day. I had plans for the next phase of growth and had mapped out the strategy to do this. I knew exactly the steps I needed to take, and exactly when to take them, in order to get there. All I had to do was implement them. However, when I looked ahead, all I saw was a long road with lots of work—and few surprises. I had the roadmap but I needed to run what looked like a marathon in order to get to the finish line.

It was hard to get excited. I realised that I'd lost my passion for my business, something I thought would never happen. I resigned myself to the fact that this must happen to entrepreneurs once they reached a certain stage of growth. Should I recruit a general manager and walk away—participating only from afar? Should I sell up? Should I try to revive that early excitement by starting something new? I began researching my options, and every day things just got harder. I was at a crossroads and I had to make a decision.

(E) Returning from adventure with new insight

Then I attended a business conference at which the organisers held a session that opened with one of those cheesy ice-breaking games where you have to share. I confess, I hate them. And I wasn't really in the mood to high-five the person sitting next to me or share with them the answer to whatever inane question the moderator put forward. Today it was: 'What are your top three plans for your business this year?' *Woohoo. Are we ready for that? Everyone say 'Yes!'* I was tired, I had a gruelling travel schedule and I didn't feel that talking about my business plan to a total stranger would alleviate my workload or put me in a better mood.

Then again, sometimes the universe has other plans. I put on my best 'polite' face and went through the motions just so we could get the ice-breaker over and done with. I was sitting next to Jo, as her name badge loudly proclaimed. I told her my plans for the year and then added: 'I guess I'm fortunate enough to be at a point in my business where it's solid. And I just need to implement the strategy I've mapped out. Maybe it's unrealistic to think you can have the same level of excitement you once had when it was all shiny and new. This feeling probably happens to everyone who has been in business for a while. You can't stay excited about it forever.'

Jo didn't try to agree or disagree with this comment. Instead, she simply asked: 'What did you used to get excited about?'

I replied: 'I'm passionate about helping people achieve what they've always wanted, whatever that might be. I get excited when people accomplish things they once didn't think possible. In my business, that's their writing goals. People get published, they get book deals and they get promoted when their writing skills improve.'

Jo asked: 'So does that still happen in your business, even after six years?'

I said: 'Yes, actually it happens more than ever now, just because we serve so many more people than we used to.'

Jo didn't say anything. She just looked at me, waiting for the words to sink in. I realised that I had been so caught up in the daily grind of my business, so engrossed in the strategy I had in place, that I'd lost touch with why I went into business in the first place.

The minute I remembered why I was doing this, I could actually feel the sense of drudgery dissipating. I could feel a smile return. I thought of the students who have found themselves with publishing contracts or new careers as a result of doing our courses and how excited they were to get paid to write. I realised that in the midst of the grind of administration, operations, implementation and the mile-long 'to do' list that face most business owners, I had to make a point of reminding myself of why I was really doing this.

The story I told myself—about being stuck in Groundhog Day and pushing forward through a limitless sea of administrative challenges—had a huge (negative) impact. But I had to remember that there was another story I should be telling myself—about the lives that had been transformed because of what we do.

Instead of just making a mental note of this from time to time, I took practical steps to make sure it was in my face every day. I started a private closed Facebook group that only graduates could join. It was one of the best things I've done. Every day I dip into the group to find students sharing stories about their successes. It's a constant positive reminder of why I do what I do. It's also become a great 'listening post'. Observing the discussions in this community helps me realise what people want in terms of new products and services.

The sequel

Well, like many good stories, of course there's a sequel. And this time it involves characters from all over the world. We're already seeing students enrolling in our online courses from Canada, the US, UK, Asia, Europe, the Middle East ... everywhere. So the next part of the story is about consolidating our position as one of the world's leading writers' centres. We still have a long way to go, and if you want to see if we make it…well, you'll just have to stay tuned for the rest of the story.

Spark to flame to fire

Now that might seem like a long story, but I've told you the extended version so you can get some idea of my background. When I meet someone for the first time, I don't launch into a monologue about my life story at the first opportunity. Too much information. I pick and choose the right time to share my stories.

You need to know your own story intimately so you can draw on it when it's most effective. Take the time to document it, because it will be well worth your effort. You'll use different versions, in varying lengths, at different times.

Imagine your stories having different levels of intensity. You can start with the spark of an idea and, if you've crafted it well, it may well intrigue someone enough to investigate it. A spark catches into a flame, and your story grows ever so slightly. And then, if your listener or audience wants to find out more, the flame bursts into a fire.

You want to fan this interest so you're able to expand on your story and reveal more of yourself. Specifically, you want to share the parts of your story that are most relevant to the person you're communicating with. The more engaged people become, the more likely they will share your story with others. Like a fire, it spreads naturally and you won't have to work so hard to make it happen.

If you feel resistant to documenting your own entrepreneur's journey, remember that it's not set in stone. You're the author. That means you can edit it, deleting or adding events when needed. Writing this down now doesn't mean you have to stick with telling this version of your journey forever. The key to this exercise is to identify different incidents, turning points and lessons that have been a part of your journey so far. You can download the template whenever you want to do this exercise again, until you feel you've nailed it.

As you decide what events or experiences to include in each key section of the template, you'll discover the ones that work—and the ones that don't seem to fit. Your entrepreneur's journey has the potential to be one of the most rewarding adventures of your life. Take the time to tell it.

Your actions

Your entrepreneur's journey

1 Download your Entrepreneur's Journey template in the exclusive resources section at <www.powerstoriesbook.com> or simply use the categories listed in table 2.1 (on p. 17).
2 Fill in the key events, turning points and lessons for each section. Remember to write this from your own perspective as entrepreneur. Don't be afraid to get personal. You can always edit later.
3 Once you've written down as much as you can remember, leave it for an hour or a day. Then come back and look at it through fresh eyes.
4 Review your narrative from the beginning to the point reached in your journey so far. What's jarring? What doesn't make sense? What are you uncomfortable about? Edit your story so it's succinct and feels 'whole'.
5 Keep this story, but don't be afraid to change it if you feel you can make it more interesting, moving or inspiring. I don't mean you should fabricate anything but, rather, you'll discover the anecdotes and experiences that resonate with people—and those that fall flat. Edit accordingly.

The point of this exercise is to familiarise yourself with your own story. This is the framework on which your eight power stories are built. The clearer you are on your own entrepreneur's journey, the easier it will be to identify the unique power stories that are going to make you shine.

CHAPTER 3

Your passion story

Walking frames. When I first met business owner Sue Chen, I found out that she made walking frames and canes. I'll confess: this did not excite me.

We were at a global event for female entrepreneurs in Rio de Janeiro when the speaker invited Sue on stage for an impromptu talk about her business. Since I've never been interested in walking frames—and I don't know anyone who is—I opened my laptop and hoped I looked like I was taking notes as I began checking my email. But I didn't get very far into my inbox before I found myself being drawn into Sue's story. Not only did she manage to get me more than a little interested in walking frames, but by the end of her two-minute spiel I practically wanted one.

So what was so engaging about Sue's story? Quite simply, her passion. That's the first power story you need in your arsenal. Your Passion Story.

This is the story that informs people—from your customers and prospects to your staff and suppliers—what you're passionate about.

This story goes beyond explaining your qualifications and your technical skills, beyond labels like 'engineer', 'chiropractor', 'wine connoisseur' and 'triathlete'. This is the story that explains the 'why' behind what gets you out of bed every morning.

When you can identify and communicate this 'why', your enthusiasm is infectious. People can see that spark in your eye. They can tell when you're truly passionate about something. They can also tell when you're *not* passionate about something. It's an emotion you just can't fake.

With a broad California twang Sue speaks passionately about what she does. 'When I meet someone and they ask me what I do, I say: "I make beautiful canes and hot turbo walkers!"' she declares.

Sue founded her business, Nova, when she was just 23, straight after graduating from college. With no background in science or medicine, Sue created the company to help her family. Her grandfather and three uncles lived in Taiwan and ran a factory they co-founded with Sue's father, who had migrated to the US when Sue was four years old. He died of cancer when she was 14. The factory manufactured walking frames and canes for other medical product companies, but it didn't sell under its own brand. Sue's grandfather decided that had to change, and it was going to be Sue's job to make that happen.

'I felt really proud that my grandfather had faith in me,' says Sue. 'Especially since he came from a different era. My uncles weren't so keen. They wanted to partner with a US company to distribute our products.' After frustrating attempts to strike up the right partnerships, Sue's grandfather threw up his hands in despair. She recalls: 'My grandfather just said, "Forget it. No more partners." He looked at me and said, "You start the company."

'At the time I had no clue. I didn't even know how to incorporate a company,' she says. 'I remember going to our first trade show and I was so overwhelmed. It was dominated by middle-aged men in grey suits. I thought: "How in the world am I going to make a difference here?" We didn't make a single sale.'

After this unpromising start, Sue began learning all she could about the industry. In 1994 she managed to bring in $72 000 in revenue. By 2011 she was named by *Fortune* magazine as one of 10 Most Powerful Women Entrepreneurs in the US. Her goal is to turn over $28 million in 2012.

When Sue first started the company, she sold the standard grey walkers that other providers were already supplying the industry. 'They were everywhere—and they were horrible. They were hard to move because to go forward you had to pick them up and shuffle a couple of steps each time. It took forever just to walk across the room. And then people would try to make them easier to push by sticking tennis balls on to the bottom. Those walkers were so ugly!'

The more time Sue spent with patients with mobility issues, the more she realised how inadequate these walkers were, not only in functionality but also in style. That's right, style. 'There was no innovation in this industry,' she says. 'Everyone was making the same products they had been for years, including us. The same walkers, the same canes.'

Sue decided to try something different. With the standard grey walker dominating the US market, she ordered a shipment of walkers more popular in Europe. They were blue and featured wheels so they were easier to push and a seat in case the user got tired. 'I thought it was a great product but no-one wanted it. I tried and tried and tried. But we just couldn't sell it.' Sue literally had to give them away, and began placing them in places frequented by people with mobility difficulties, such as rehabilitation centres and hospitals.

Soon afterwards Yolanda walked into Sue's life. And that was when Sue really became passionate about her business. At the time, Yolanda was 60 years old and couldn't walk 10 steps. She had gained weight, become depressed and hardly left her house, cut off from family and friends. But then she discovered the new blue walker, and it transformed her life. 'I remember it like it was yesterday,' Sue says. 'Here was this spunky woman who was energetic and funny. She told me the story about how the walker had changed everything.

'We talked about her life, her kids and her grandkids. She'd point to her behind and say: "My butt used to be so much bigger and look at it now. I'm walking a mile a day, and I've lost 30 pounds. I can do anything that I was doing before, and the most important thing is that I'm back to being myself again."

'She was such a dynamic and sassy lady that I couldn't have even imagined her with the old grey walking frame, shuffling along because it had no wheels. I loved her attitude, but it was sad to know that when she lost her mobility that spunkiness and passion went away. That was a turning point for me because I realised that people like Yolanda not only need a functional walker, they probably want one that looks good, too. People often choose their cars to suit their tastes and personality. Why not their walkers and canes?'

Sue was committed to making that happen. By then, Yolanda wasn't the only person who had discovered Sue's walker. Her idea of giving it away free to rehab centres and hospitals meant that patients would come across it. The phone started to ring. With access to her family's factory in Taiwan, she began to design and create walkers with a difference. She introduced them in a range of colours.

'We were the first company to do that. Then other manufacturers started following our lead, which was a great thing because it helped us stay competitive. Also, an advantage of being a woman in a male-dominated industry was that I understood that people still want to have style. I look at what's coming into fashion. I go to the Gucci website. I look at Coach and Prada. I get ideas of what's coming, because why shouldn't the newest trends in designer bags be something that I use to inspire the bags on our walkers?'

Apart from introducing colours and funky patterns in walkers and canes, Sue also made a point of listening to as many of her customers' stories as possible. The seat is too small? Sue makes a bigger seat. Nowhere to hang your handbag? Add a basket. Need a cup-holder? Consider it done. Want an accessible pocket on the side of the frame? Choose from these stylish prints and patterns. Too heavy to lift into the car? Let's change the metal and reduce the weight by half.

'I have more passion now than I did when I started,' she says. 'I get to spend time with these amazing people. Being out there and hearing the stories of my customers—it keeps us alive and innovative as a company. Whenever I feel like I'm burning out, which happens when you're an entrepreneur, I remind myself who I serve. I get back out there, get out of my office, away from my desk—the mounds of paper and the endless emails that never go away—and it always sets me straight when people share their stories with me about how Nova has made a difference in their life. Then, boom! That passion comes right back, and it's even greater than before.'

Why is your passion story so important?

Let's face it. In most cases, people get excited when they deal with someone who is truly passionate. It's infectious. It's not that they necessarily share the *same* passion or interest as you, although if that happens it's a bonus. They may not even understand the idea you're so keen on. In fact, they don't have to relate to the object of your passion at all. But they do connect with the fact that you *have* a passion — something that ignites your imagination, makes you smile and gives you a purpose or motivation.

When you share your passion with someone else, they identify with you (a) because they understand what it feels like to be passionate about a cause, idea or activity, or (b) because *they wish they could feel this way themselves*. People crave this feeling of purpose and direction, and they can relate to it when they recognise it in someone else. It's a fundamental part of the entrepreneur's journey. And that's why it's one of your power stories.

In Sue Chen's case, it's not just about her journey in building her business and transforming her industry, it's also about her internal journey: how a 23-year-old woman could take on an established industry predominantly run by middle-aged men ... and triumph, not only in building a successful business but also in transforming people's lives along the way.

What is your passion story?

Think about your passion story. The better you know it, the better it will sound next time you tell it. Remember, you rarely launch into a long tale about all the things that make you passionate about what you do. You start with a spark, something that will intrigue people. Once they're drawn in, it bursts into flame, and then you can fan it with more details about your story until it becomes a fire.

Here are three strategies you should have ready to go.

The spark

The key here is to spark the interest of the person you're talking to. You want to provide information about yourself in an easily digestible way that intrigues them enough to want to know more.

Focus on: describing your passion

Depending on the circumstances, you might use this when you meet people for the first time or when you have only a short time in which to explain who you are and what you do.

Try this: I love [describe your passion]. I love doing this because [talk about what excites you and what you find rewarding about it]. The best part is [describe an outcome of what you do].

Example: I love helping people who want to get published, improve their writing or change careers to become a writer. I love doing this because there's nothing more rewarding than seeing people realise this is possible. The best part is when they actually take those steps and I can see that it's changed their life.

Take a few minutes to write your version now.

So how does this differ from your elevator pitch—your 10- to 30-second spiel about what you do and what your business is about? We'll go into detail about your elevator pitch in the next chapter. There is definitely a subtle difference. But don't overthink it. You don't want to get into an internal debate about which pitch to pull out every time you meet someone. You'll wind up tongue-tied as your brain tosses up which one to use. Trust your gut. And tell whichever power story comes most naturally to the conversation you're having at the time.

If you're interacting in a more formal or corporate environment, you may choose to use your elevator pitch about your business. Let's say you've bumped into the chief financial officer of a major multinational company during the coffee break at their annual general meeting. Chances are this won't be the ideal moment to share your passion story. But if you met them in a social setting—say, at an informal networking drinks session—that could be perfect.

The flame

Now it's time to turn that spark of your story into a flame. But when you're still getting to know someone, you want a slow comfortable burn so that people aren't overwhelmed with too much information.

Focus on: how you help others

After you spark people's interest, they'll typically ask a follow-up question, such as: 'How do you do that?' This is the perfect opportunity to turn the spark of your story into a 'flame'.

Try this: I do this by [succinctly describe the way in which you achieve the outcomes described in the 'spark'].

Example: I do this by running short courses in many different types of writing. So whether you want to write a novel, a screenplay, a business book or a media release, you can discover exactly how to do this through one of our courses, which can be taken online or in person, at the Sydney Writers' Centre.

The key here is not to go into too much detail. You don't want listeners to suffer from information overload. That's why it's important to refine your 'flame' so it's short and succinct. You want to pique people's interest so they ask you for more information. You don't want their eyes to glaze over.

The fire

Now you want to fan that flame so it turns into a fire. This is when you get to tell other aspects of your story and give other people a real insight into your business, passions and life.

Focus on: conversation

Once people are engaged in a deeper conversation with you about your story, this is where you'll reveal some or part of your entrepreneur's journey (which you identified in the previous chapter). This could happen at a dinner party; or you might be questioned by a job applicant you're interviewing; or maybe you're pitching to investors and they want to hear more about your story than what's revealed in the budget forecasts you've given them.

Again, don't get caught up in wondering which part you should reveal when. Just treat it as a conversation and bring up the points you think most relevant and interesting at the time. Like a fire, your story can glow subtly or burn intensely. It's up to you to fan it when you feel the time is right and to pull back when it's time to talk about something else. You can draw on different elements and showcase different aspects of your experience to suit the circumstances.

If I'm giving a one-hour keynote presentation about how you can achieve your dreams, you might hear most of that story. Among business owners on Twitter, I might give brief examples of our challenges and how we overcame them, or I might respond to someone else's tweet by sharing a photo or link to illustrate what I'm passionate about.

To call on the right parts of your story when you need them, however, you need to be clear on what your story is. That's why identifying the various parts of your passion story is so important.

Don't have passion for your business?

If you're clear on what you're passionate about, this exercise is going to be very easy. But what if you're not really that passionate about your business, or if you're struggling to identify how your passions connect with your business? Don't worry. Your passions are probably there, bubbling below the surface, but are simply covered by layers of … life — that is, responsibilities, children, relationships, studies, other people's expectations and all the things you think you *should* do, instead of the things you'd simply *love* to do.

Business coach Ali Brown points out that entrepreneurs sometimes 'fall into' their businesses. Based in Los Angeles, Ali coaches business owners around the world, including in the UK, Australia and Asia. She was named one of Ernst & Young's Winning Women Entrepreneurs in 2010 and was featured on the ABC television show *The Secret Millionaire* in 2011. Ali says she often sees people go into business simply because they have a particular skill, whether dog grooming or sales training or IT maintenance. 'When you're skilled at something, it can be tempting to open a business based around that skill,' says Ali. 'On paper, that might make sense. However, you could also end up with a business you're not actually passionate about.'

Without a passionate connection to your business, it will be hard to maintain your enthusiasm for it. And that is palpable when you're talking to other people, whether they are customers, employees, investors or suppliers. So it's worth taking the time to identify what you are passionate about. To start figuring this out, Ali says: 'Ask yourself: "What did I love to do when I was 12 years old?"' It sounds like such a simple question. But it will help you get to the core of what you want to identify.

When I was 12, I was in Mrs Heath's history class. I was supposed to be studying the Renaissance. For my assignment I created an olde worlde version of *Cosmopolitan* magazine. Long before the days of desktop publishing and iPad apps that can create magazines with a few swipes and some Flickr photos, I was creating them the old-fashioned way, with my dad's typewriter (we didn't have a computer yet), cut-up photos (there was no Instagram back then either), glue and staples. Every article was a story about the Renaissance — *Cosmo*-style. Even back then I loved telling stories.

Mrs Heath, on the other hand, didn't see it the same way. She failed me on that assignment. She said I got top marks for presentation but felt that the tabloid-style treatment of my stories was 'not appropriate'. Of course, I thought that was grossly unfair. But I loved the process of putting together a magazine, even though I'll admit my efforts did look a bit crap, and I secretly hoped I would be able to do it one day for real.

What got you excited when you were young? What did you absolutely love to do in your spare time? What were you passionate about when you weren't encumbered with a job, mortgage, kids and other responsibilities. This will usually give a very strong clue to what your true passions are.

I know there are many other more comprehensive techniques to determine your passions. You can visit a careers or life coach and write copious lists of the activities you enjoy, your hobbies, interests, values and so on. And if you have the time to do that, then go for it. But I agree with Ali's suggestion. The quick hack on this is to simply ask yourself: 'What did I love to do when I was 12 years old?'

Dig deep — it's there

I once had to interview a number of accountants for a series I was writing for a business magazine. Now, I know accountants have long been the butt of jokes the world over. They are painted as boring, dull, lifeless nerds with calculators in their top pockets, and number-crunching may not be the most exciting activity in the world. But the power of story was brought home to me when I interviewed two very different accountants, both equity partners in their own firms, and had to choose which of the two to feature in my article.

When I asked the first accountant (we'll call him Bill) why he was drawn to the profession, he said: 'Oh, I tell people they shouldn't do accounting. I don't know why people want to do it. When I meet university graduates, the young people tell me: "I'm keen to be an accountant..." But I just don't get it. I can understand young people saying they want to be a neurosurgeon or a fireman or a policeman. But an *accountant*? Who actually *wants* to do that?

'I didn't have a burning passion to study accounting when I first started out. My dad was an accountant and so was my brother, so I just did it because that's what they did. I don't regret it though. I'm good at what I do, and so is everyone in my firm. Our clients know that when we work on their projects, they'll get excellent advice.

'When I tell people they shouldn't do accounting, I say that with tongue in cheek. But I really do secretly wonder why any young person would actually find it interesting.'

I was surprised by Bill's attitude. This wasn't a heart-to-heart with a colleague. He was talking to me as a representative of his firm. I was interviewing him for an article about careers in accounting. And he knew this.

Bill didn't exactly overflow with passion for his chosen career, and ordinarily that's fine. We don't all have to bubble over with enthusiasm about our jobs. But Bill was letting his company, and himself, down with his story. Maybe he thought he was being funny. Maybe he was just telling the truth. Maybe he was just unaware that he wasn't leaving a particularly positive impression. Whatever the reason, he painted a certain picture of himself and his firm.

This was a far cry from my interview with another accountant we'll call Kevin, who was also a partner in his accounting firm. When I asked Kevin the same question he replied: 'I love the fact that I help people make better decisions. It's not just about the numbers. It's not about balance sheets and financial reports. They are just the technical tools we use. The technical aspect is fulfilling in itself, because I find that side of it intellectually stimulating. But I like the way this job gives me an opportunity to make a difference in the decisions made by my clients, and hopefully they have a more successful business as a result of my input.

'As a chartered accountant, I really believe that one of the best ways you can serve people is by helping them. You help them make more informed decisions. You equip them with accurate information so they can make wise choices. That way, they get a better outcome. And that's how we, as a country, can improve across all industries. After all, isn't that what we should be doing? Making sure that each generation has a better world to live in than the one before.'

Kevin spoke with a genuine passion that was palpable, whereas you could tell that Bill just wanted to be somewhere else. Bill went through the motions and tried to put forward some positive points about the accounting profession, but it was obvious he didn't believe in his own words.

Kevin and Bill. Chalk and cheese. The difference: a passion story. Kevin has nailed his. Bill hasn't.

It's important to note that Bill doesn't have to make one up. He shouldn't feign excitement about his career if he genuinely isn't thrilled by it. But he should try to identify what *does* get him excited. Why did he become a partner in an accounting practice in the first place? When I asked him what gets him out of bed in the morning and makes him keen to get to work, Bill slowly began to identify what drives him.

He told me: 'The area of accounting I love most is forensic accounting. Here we investigate the financial aspects of certain insurance claims, fraud, misuse of funds and so on. Every matter is unique. There's a methodology in how we do our job but because every case is different, you have to look at the big picture and see how you're going to tackle it. I'm never bored. It's like the thriller stories I used to read when I was younger. There was always a problem to solve or a villain to bring down. Our cases are usually quite complex and challenging. It's exciting. It's like James Bond meets *CSI*, except you're an accountant.'

Finally speaking about his passion, Bill had suddenly become a lot more interesting. Those were his exact words. He had finally identified what drove him in his business. The trouble is that many people don't take the time to identify what they are passionate about, and therefore they rarely articulate it. Bill had been recycling his story about being a boring accountant when his work was actually far from boring. He just bought into the common perception of accountants as having less than thrilling careers compared with neurosurgeons or firemen.

Chances are you *can* actually connect your passion with your work. It just might not be the most obvious link. Too often we make the mistake of thinking that we have to sound passionate about our business or job, that we have to sound enthusiastic about what we do every day. But if this story isn't genuine we shouldn't be telling it, because it won't be convincing. The key is to identify what you are authentically passionate about and then *determine how that fits in with your job or business. That's* the story you need to be telling.

Making a difference

Fotini Hatzis is a hair and makeup artist in Australia. In her private salon in inner-city Melbourne, she's surrounded by massive gilt-framed mirrors, and she moves from client to client with the confidence and expertise of a veteran with 26 years' experience. Over that time her clientele has evolved to include some of Australia's top celebrities. She also works with private clients, who pay top dollar for her advice. Typically these are time-poor corporate women who have money to burn and don't want to be seen at the makeup counter of the local department store getting advice from a 16-year-old shop assistant who can't even apply her own makeup properly.

While her clientele may have changed over the past two decades, the actual work Fotini does hasn't really evolved that much. Of course, she regularly adapts to different hair and makeup trends but, let's face it, there's only so much innovation that can happen in the world of brushes, powders and eye-liners.

When I asked her what she truly loves, what she's really passionate about, Fotini doesn't bang on about the latest mascara from Givenchy or the quality of the foundation from Armani. She's doesn't wax lyrical about how to get hair like Beyonce. She talks about transforming people's confidence.

'I love it when I can see that I've made a difference in someone's life,' she said. 'When women do workshops with me, I get them to bring in their own makeup so we're using what they already have. When it comes to makeup, less is often more, but it just needs to be applied in the right way. People want to look natural and feel beautiful. It's not how good you make someone look. It's how good you make them feel.

'Some women walk out transformed. You can see how happy and confident they are. They might seem like successful business women but the change in their self-esteem can be enormous, and long-lasting, when they become more confident about how they look. That's what I love—when I know I've made a difference.'

That's what drives Fotini. Making a difference. Seeing other women become more confident as a result of her advice. That's what her passion is. Not the makeup or the curlers or the fancy things you can do with the GHD hair straightener, but the positive impact she can make on another person.

Think about what gets you excited about what you do. What gets you out of bed everyday? Is it the people you meet, the challenge of problem-solving, the fact you can make a difference to someone's life? It may not have anything to do with your skills or the tools of your trade. It's the passion that drives you to do what you do.

Why you need to share your passion story

Your passion might be flying kites, creating stories or restoring vintage cars, or it might be changing people's lives. Everyone is different. If it's connected to the work you do, great. It makes sense for you to share your story so people get an understanding about what inspires and drives you.

You might think that people won't be interested in your passion. It's true that your story will resonate with different people on different levels and to different degrees. That's perfectly natural. But don't be afraid to share your passion story just because you think some people aren't going to embrace it. The people you meet aren't mind-readers, so you need to be proactive in sharing your story to attract those who can actually help you pursue your passion. How can others help you on your journey if you don't share what's important to you? By the same token, don't bang on about it ad nauseam. You need to strike the right balance.

Look, I'm the world's biggest Bon Jovi fan. There, I said it. It's my secret passion. Okay, it's not that secret. I quite happily discuss this at most available opportunities. Don't get me wrong, I don't break out into the chorus of *Living on a Prayer* during board meetings. Nor do I recite scenes from movies in which Jon Bon Jovi has starred when I'm chatting to CEOs. I mean, I know how to be professional. But Jon Bon Jovi and I... well, we go way back. I've been a fan for... *decades* and I don't mind telling people about it. I'm a walking cliché when it comes to my Bon Jovi obsession.

So picture this. I was sitting at my computer one day, in the depths of a corporate writing project for an insurance client, when a message pops into my inbox: *Can you interview Bon Jovi for us next week? You also need to follow the band around for the day and you get VIP seats so you can review the concert.*

I blinked and stared at the screen. I must have been hallucinating. Or perhaps I was delirious. I blinked again and read the email s-l-o-w-l-y just in case I was suffering from some new kind of dyslexia. By this time, my heart was beating so fast I thought I was going to pass out.

Needless to say, I said yes. And yes I hung out with the band, talked at length with my idol and followed them around for the day. As an added bonus, I got to dance on stage facing a stadium crowd of 50 000 fans.

But why was I asked to write about one of the biggest bands in the world when there were any number of entertainment reporters who could have done the job? Quite simply, passion. The editor commissioning the story understood that I was a fan, knew I had the writing skills, and correctly assumed that I would have a wealth of background information and previous concert experience I could draw on. Most important, she was confident I would do the job professionally and would not mutate into a screaming teenager when I met my idol. (Yes, the temptation was there. No, I did not give in to it.)

The point is, I would never have been asked to do the interview if I hadn't previously broadcast my passion.

Use this power story. Share your passion story with others. When you share your passion with others, they can see you're bringing something extra to the table. You're bringing more than just your technical skills, you're bringing a chutzpah that can make all the difference.

Whether you allude to it in your tweets or your blog posts or elaborate on it in a keynote presentation, the act of sharing your passion will help you make that all-important emotional connection with others.

Your passion story is often intrinsically linked to the call to adventure on your entrepreneur's journey. When you let other people share your entrepreneurial journey, you not only empower them to help you pursue your passions, you open the door to opportunities that may have once seemed out of reach.

Your actions

Your passion story

Pour yourself a glass of wine or a cup of coffee, get a notepad and step away from your computer. You don't want to be distracted by emails, tweets or items on your 'to do' list that are calling your name. You want to dig deep and think about what you are truly passionate about. This is going to form the core of your passion story.

Follow these steps or download your Passion Story template in the exclusive resources section at <www.powerstoriesbook.com>.

1 Write down what you are truly passionate about and describe how it drives your business.
2 Explain how this passion helps other people.
3 If you don't feel passionate about your business, ask yourself: What did I love to do when I was 12 years old? Connect that passion with what you currently do.
4 Identify situations, either in real life or online, in which you can share your passion story.

CHAPTER 4

Your business story

Chicken. They always seem to serve chicken at networking events. The meal choice least likely to offend people's palates. There's roast chicken, marsala chicken, or, if it's at a fancier venue, maybe even chicken stuffed with feta and spinach wrapped in prosciutto. If there's one thing that's almost as sure as getting chicken at a networking function, it's hearing a bunch of stunningly forgettable elevator pitches. Even worse are the ones that actually damage the reputation a business owner has worked so hard to build. Don't let yours be one of them.

Of course, some people have their elevator pitches down to a fine art. But I'm amazed at the number of business owners who have given little or no thought to explaining what they do. This is why it's so important to take the time to craft another important power story: your Business Story.

This is quite different from your *passion* story, which is rooted in emotion. Your business story relies more on tangible facts, but you still need to be able to tell it in an engaging and interesting way, to make it resonate with people in the same way as your passion story.

Quite simply, your business story paints a clear picture of what your business is about. The key word here is 'clear'. Too often, I see entrepreneurs cloak their business story in layers of information that only detract from their core message.

Not long ago, I was at a networking dinner where everyone in the room stood up and introduced themselves to the room. One woman (we'll call her Laura) stood up and said:

> 'Hi, my name is Laura. I'm a business coach and I work with small business owners and solopreneurs. I'm part of a worldwide network of more than 1100 certified coaches in 67 countries around the world. We share resources and I just returned from our international conference in Paris.'

Even as she was saying it, I could see people's eyes glaze over, their attention slipping away. The chicken was decidedly more interesting.

Laura had it all wrong. If her clients are small business owners, then it's very unlikely they will ever want to tap into the resources provided by the other 1100 certified coaches in her network. And they couldn't care less about whether she went to a conference in Paris, Geneva or Hong Kong. They are more likely to want to find a locally based business coach who is keen to invest the time to get to know their specific needs.

Boasting about a 'worldwide network' might be useful if you're an international courier company. Or if you want to target clients who themselves have offices around the globe and need the support of a supplier who can offer that coverage. But Laura's elevator pitch didn't resonate with many of the people in the room.

What could she have done to improve her story? That depends on what she specialises in, but perhaps:

> 'Hi, my name is Laura. I'm a business coach and I help small business owners and solopreneurs improve their profitability, get more customers and reduce the time they need to spend on their business.'

Your 10-second elevator pitch

Your 10-second elevator pitch explains who you are and what you do in the time it would take to … ride 10 seconds in an elevator.

Focus on: who and what

Picture this. You get into the elevator with someone, you explain what you do and then you have to get out again, because you've reached your floor. You may never see that person again, but you want them to remember you, *so make every word count.*

Your aim is to intrigue that person enough that they want to get out of the elevator with you to find out more about what you do. While it might seem that an elevator pitch is all about you, in fact the smartest elevator pitches are the ones that focus on who you can help.

So what's your 10-second elevator pitch? What story are you telling people you meet? Are you finding that people politely excuse themselves to 'go find a drink' or do you intrigue people enough for them to say, 'Tell me more.' If you haven't crafted your elevator pitch yet, take the time to write it down now.

Try this: My name is [insert your name]. I run/am [insert the kind of business you run or explain your expertise]. I help [explain the kind of people you help].

Example: My name is Valerie Khoo. I run Australia's leading centre for writing courses. We help people who want to get published and write with confidence.

I keep it short and sharp. When you are meeting someone for the first time at a function or conference, you don't want to give them your life history. You don't want to be the person at networking functions with the reputation for telling long-winded self-serving stories. Don't bombard people with your résumé. Intrigue people with key information so they want to discover more about you.

But it doesn't end there. The aim is to generate enough interest from others to stir that initial spark into a flame. So that brings us to …

Your 30-second pitch

In your 10-second pitch, you focus on the basics: who you are and what you do. If you've done a good job, you should hear the magic words: 'Tell me more' or 'How do you do that?' So you need to have this follow-up explanation ready to go. In the 30-second version, you can build on your basic pitch by explaining 'how' you help people.

Focus on: how

You should have already nailed your 'how' pitch in the previous chapter, so just use the same construction. If not, craft it now.

Try this: I do this by [succinctly describe how your business helps people].

Example: We do this by offering short courses in different types of writing. So whether you want or write a novel, a screenplay, a business book or a media release, you can discover exactly how to do that through one of our courses, which can be taken online or in person.

Note the use of 'I' or 'we' here. Often they're interchangeable. If I'm talking about my business, I'll probably use 'we'. If I'm talking about my personal passion, I'll use 'I'.

When you're confident in your elevator speech and your message is clear and concise, you'll make an impression. Even if people don't need your services right away, you want them to remember you for when they are ready to buy or refer you on.

Here's a further example of an elevator speech that works. While I was attending another networking event that had the same tradition of encouraging everyone to stand up and introduce themselves to the room, one woman got up and said:

'Hello, my name is Patricia. I run a family law practice and I typically help people who are going through divorce. This is a difficult time in anyone's life and I help my clients when they are often emotional, stressed and drained. My clients are usually women and, in particular, I make sure that their spouse is not hiding any assets or trying to get out of a fair divorce arrangement. I fight for my clients. I don't take shit from anyone. I won't give up. I hope to God that you never have to use the services of someone like me but, if you do, you want me on *your* side.'

Patricia was confident and direct, and made sure she made eye contact with as many people in the room as she could. Compared with Laura's vague elevator speech, which focused less on how she could help people than on irrelevant numbers and conference destinations, Patricia nailed hers.

You'll see that Patricia follows this pattern:

My name is [insert your name].	Hello, my name is Patricia.
I run/am [insert the kind of business you run or explain your expertise].	I run a family law practice.
I help [explain how you help people].	I typically help people who are going through divorce. This is a difficult time in anyone's life and I help my clients when they are often emotional, stressed and drained. My clients are usually women.
I do this by [succinctly describe how your business helps people].	In particular, I make sure that their spouse is not hiding any assets or trying to get out of a fair divorce arrangement. I fight for my clients. I don't take shit from anyone. I won't give up. I hope to God that you never have to use the services of someone like myself but, if you do, you want me on *your* side.

You don't need to be as bold as Patricia in your elevator speech but you do need to be direct.

Of course, your elevator pitch isn't the only place you'll tell your business story. You're likely to feature a version of it on your website and marketing materials such as brochures or flyers. You might also include a version in your social media profile. If you're using social media for business purposes, then remember that your profile is one of the key elements in helping people decide whether or not to 'follow' you. While it's fine to pepper your profile with quirky observations like 'Loves red wine' or 'Often found indulging in chocolate and whisky', you also need to ensure you have enough information in your profile so people understand who you are and what you do.

Get to the point

The biggest mistake I see entrepreneurs make when telling their business story is that they take far too long to get to the point. In today's fast-paced world, people are bombarded with messages — advertising, emails, marketing, signs, jingles, commercials, the list is endless. Chances are that when they are confronted with your business story (in whatever form), they aren't in the mood to drink it in like a velvety glass of merlot. It's unlikely that they've turned off the television and logged off their email just so they can savour the words on your website. They're probably not as receptive to your story as they would be to their favourite novel. Instead, they're busy, juggling different tasks, toggling between screens and thinking about tomorrow's to-do list. So it's important to get to the point.

I once visited the website of a business that makes eco-friendly office chairs. The business was a pioneer in the industry, but the owners found it challenging to convince other businesses to care about the environment as much as they did. I soon realised why.

As a journalist, I interviewed the owners (we'll call them Dave and Melanie) and researched the company. When I visited the website, these were the only words on their home page:

Living Green

Committing to environmental decisions now so your children have a future

In February 2005 greenwashing was taking Australia by storm. According to the *Macquarie Dictionary*, greenwashing is 'deceptive corporate advertising designed to portray the company as caring for the environment'. Companies began to recycle. They claimed to use 'all natural products' and told customers they had a zero carbon footprint. They asserted that they complied to green standards, but these guidelines were complicated and the rules hard to navigate. We wanted to ensure that we provided a transparent manufacturing process to show cradle-to-grave product stewardship. We wanted to 'close the loop', and so we started on the path to ensuring that all our products could truly be called 'green'. We are committed to full environmental certification.

Really? What about some information about what the business actually does? I began to wonder whether they were a chair manufacturer or a lobby group. After interviewing Dave and Melanie, it was obvious they were passionate about the environment. They had applied rigorous tests and made significant changes to their business in order to comply with various well-recognised eco-certification programs.

But they had no idea how to tell their business story. They could have featured a message as simple as:

> We manufacture and customise eco-friendly office chairs. We'll help you minimise your impact on the environment with affordable solutions in a wide range of colours and textiles.

Dave and Melanie explained that they wanted to make it clear to customers that they were serious about their environmental credentials. They didn't want people to think they were 'greenwashing' or misleading anyone. However, displaying a definition of 'greenwashing' as the first message on their website served only to confuse people. They could have displayed their commitment to the environment by telling their story, describing how they became passionate about it. By explaining how they motivated their employees to get behind it. By showcasing how they pivoted their business from a regular chair manufacturing company to one that now provides only environmentally friendly chairs.

Instead, the entire website was full of environmental jargon, replete with acronyms, references to organisations most people would never have heard of, and not a single mention of Dave and Melanie. Instead, 'we' was used throughout:

- 'We are committed to quality ... '
- 'We selected partners with the greatest potential to change ... '
- 'We engaged the services of EOAL to test all fabrics for carbon emissions ... '

There is nothing wrong with using 'we'. The mistake was that Dave and Melanie's role in the organisation—as owners, founders and active leaders—did not rate a single mention. They were invisible. I sometimes hear business owners say, 'Oh but it's not about me. It's about the team. I don't want to mention individual names. I want people to know it's a team effort.' And when I do, I just shake my head. Please. Get real and join the trust economy. People want to know that there is a captain on the ship. Consumers want to know there are real people they can trust behind the decisions of a company, especially in a start-up or any small to medium-sized business. They are reassured when they know they are not dealing with a faceless organisation.

When Dave and Melanie chose *not* to make an appearance in their own story they wasted an opportunity to build trust and credibility with their target audience. Who would you be more likely to believe—two people talking about their passion for the environment, or an endless series of web pages full of jargon?

Lose the flowery language

Another essential factor in getting to the point is to lose the flowery language. It can be tempting to pepper your business story with jargon and multisyllabic words in order to make it sound more important. But ultimately this just makes you sound like a total tosser. Take these examples:

> 'We focus on solutions-based problem solving.' (What other kind of freaking problem solving is there?)
> 'We'll action a needs assessment of the situation and implement a strategy to work towards our clients' goals.' (We'll find out what needs to be done to achieve what you want and do it.)
> 'It's important to innovate integrated functionalities.' (We'll add new features.)

Seriously, it would be about as meaningful to pick random words out of the dictionary and string them together. Get rid of 'empty' words and make sure you are actually conveying useful information in your story. Lose the words and phrases that will win at corporate buzzword bingo and simply use plain English. You want to communicate, not complicate.

What message are you sending people?

I know a graphic designer (we'll call him Michael) who actively markets his services to small business owners. However, like many entrepreneurs his business goes through peaks and troughs. When we last spoke, he wasn't reaching his sales targets.

'I advertise in my local newspaper, I go to networking events where there are other small business owners. I just don't seem to be getting the traction I need,' he complained. 'Sure, I get decent jobs here and there. But it's always a hard slog.'

I took a look at his website and asked him to give me his elevator pitch. It went something like this:

> 'My name's Michael and I run a full-service graphic design agency. Our clients include IBM, ING Bank, Staples, Procter & Gamble and Woolworths. If you need help in designing anything from magazines and brochures to billboards or packaging, let me know and I can give you a free quote.'

I knew immediately that he was telling the wrong story. I asked Michael why he wanted to work with small business owners. 'I like working with entrepreneurs. I like the way they think and I like working with them to bring their ideas to life,' he said. 'I also like the fact that they are usually the decision-makers. I don't have to wait till our concepts go through countless layers of approval, as they often have to in the corporate world. And often they get stalled at the board level anyway.'

I said: 'If you love working with small business owners so much, why do you highlight the likes of IBM, ING and Woolworths in your elevator pitch?'

Michael paused to think about it before answering. 'I guess it's because those clients are big names,' he said slowly. 'It makes us appear like we are credible because we've done work for them.'

I looked at him. I knew the penny would drop any second.

'Okay, I'm sending the wrong message,' he said almost sheepishly. 'I should make it explicit that I like working with small business owners.'

Not only was Michael sending confusing messages about his ideal client, he was also unwittingly sending a message about his pricing. Many small business owners would not identify with his client roster. They would never have the kind of budget of an IBM or Procter & Gamble, so they might assume his work was out of their price range.

'I've been giving that elevator pitch for so long that I never actually even listened to myself,' said Michael.

Carefully analyse what you are saying. The story you are telling may sound like it makes sense, but you might be surprised to discover what other people are actually hearing. A woman I know (we'll call her Linda) is responsible for sales and promotions at a logistics company. Over the years, I've bumped into her many times at conferences and events, and have also introduced her to a number of people. Each time, her elevator pitch is the same:

> 'My name is Linda and we're a third-party logistics company. It's my husband's business. If you ever need a third-party logistics company to help you with your drop-shipping, fulfilment or deliveries, we can help you with all that.'

I've heard her give variations of that pitch countless times, but there's one thing that never changes. That line: 'It's my husband's business.' I cringe every single time. There's nothing wrong with the fact that it's her husband's business, and there's nothing wrong with her working in it. But do you think it's an important part of her elevator pitch?

Like Michael's pitch, Linda's sends a mixed message. The subtext is: 'I'm not the decision-maker', 'I don't take ownership of what's going on.' Or even: 'I don't really want to be here but my husband asked me to come and represent the business.' Of course, Linda might simply love her husband so much and be so proud of what he has done with the business that she wants to declare it at every available opportunity. If so, that's fine. But her elevator pitch isn't the place to do it. If her goal is to find new clients, then she needs to focus on a story that's going to help others get to know, like and trust her, not confuse them with a subtext about her marriage.

Your 'About' page

One of the most common places you'll tell your business story is your 'About' page.

Focus on: telling the right story

Your 'About' or company profile page is one of the most clicked pages on your website, but how much time have you spent crafting the story you tell there? It's vital to remember that this page is a key selling tool for you and your business, so don't underestimate the power of what this page can do. It can help you establish your credibility and convince someone you're a leader in your field, and it can make or break whether you get a sale.

Are you a person or a company?

When I refer to your 'About' page, this could be 'About me' (if you are a solopreneur) or 'About us' (if you are a small business). The principles are the same. A quick caveat here, though. One mistake I see among some solopreneurs is when they try to make their business sound much bigger than it really is. When you're first starting out, I know it can be tempting to take this approach because you want to give people the impression that you're an established and thriving business with multiple staff. People do this by using statements like:

> 'Our expertise ranges from human resource consulting to running team-building leadership programs.' *(Translation: When I was an HR manager, I coordinated the office picnic and ran some courses for the senior managers.)* 'Our office is manned 24 hours a day.' *(Translation: I have a Skype number with voicemail functionality that I can access from home.)*

There's nothing wrong with being a solopreneur who aspires to grow your business. However, your customers and community generally have good bullshit meters. I encourage you to embrace the 'I' if you are indeed a solopreneur. Sure, you might not want to advertise that you work from the cupboard under the stairs or that you meet your clients in coffee shops because you don't have an office, but you don't have to pretend to run a big organisation either. People will see through the smoke and mirrors anyway.

Chances are that your clients will actually prefer the personal attention they'll get from you as a solopreneur, because they know they're not going to be palmed off to a less qualified or less experienced associate, which is more likely to happen in a larger firm.

Don't make these mistakes

Before we get into the nuts and bolts of how to create a good 'About' page for your business, let's have a look at what not to do.

Let's *not* start at the very beginning

While the famous song from *The Sound of Music* proclaims that the beginning is a very good place to start, the opposite is often true when it comes to telling your business story on your 'About' page. It can be tempting to start at the beginning. After all, that's the logical approach we were taught at school. We've been conditioned to thinking we should tell our stories in a linear fashion.

It's common to see an 'About' page start with a story about how the idea of the company came about, followed by a chronological account of the key milestones from there. This is possibly the most boring, not to mention ineffective, way to frame your company profile. Instead, start at the end. It may seem counterintuitive, but you need to remember that the reader is probably time poor, so open with a description of the core focus of your business now.

If mobile phone giant Nokia told its story chronologically, its 'About' page might sound like this:

> As Finland's leading supplier of household, consumer and military products, we manufacture footwear (including our famous rubber boots), car and bicycle tyres, plastic, aluminium, chemicals, televisions and computers, and consumer electronics.

Hardly the Nokia of today, which is synonymous with mobile phones.

Don't just replicate your résumé

If you're a solopreneur, it makes sense to incorporate some biographical elements into your 'About' page. However, remember that you still need to tell a story. You don't just want to replicate your résumé in a narrative form. There's a CEO of an IT services business in Australia (we'll call him Sam). His 'About' page starts with:

> 'Sam started his working life as a physical education teacher ...'

It then goes on to describe, in chronological order, the various positions Sam held before starting his business in IT services. Now, if Sam had started a fitness company or even a nutrition business, it might be useful to bring his background as a PE teacher to the fore, but it simply doesn't add any value to showcasing his expertise as an

IT services provider. It's not that Sam should hide this part of his life. It's just that it doesn't belong in the *first line* of his 'About' page.

Avoid too many numbers

You've heard this kind of thing before: 'We have over 200 consultants in 24 offices.' Maybe you're trying to illustrate the point that you have enough consultants to give personalised service to all customers. If that's your key message, say so:

> You'll receive personalised service and all your phone queries will be answered within one hour.

That means something to people. Telling them that your business has 200 consultants in 24 offices does not. Numbers are relative. While '200 consultants' might mean something to you, most consumers have no idea of the context unless you explain it. They don't know whether your 200 consultants are servicing 450 people or 45000 people. Put yourself in the shoes of the person who's hearing your story, and make sure any numbers you use are meaningful.

For example, let's say your business is a fitness gym. You might be happy to boast that your gym has 40 treadmills. But that number is meaningless to your prospective customers. If your point is that there are more than enough machines to go around, then say so: 'With 40 treadmills, you never have to wait for a machine.'

Similarly, you might think that it can be useful to use a number for dramatic effect. For example: '10000 children under five die in Africa every day.' It's a tragic concept. However, a number like '10000' is hard for many people to grasp. Sometimes, a more focused story can have more impact. Consider:

> At her village school, Malia's favourite subject was maths. But today her maths teacher noticed she wasn't in class. With the recent outbreak of measles among children in his village he didn't want to admit what he already knew—that he would never see Malia in his class again.

This story has a more personal and profound impact than a statistic such as '10000'. As Stalin once said: 'When one man dies it is a tragedy, when thousands die it's statistics.' You want people to *feel* tragedy, not risk them glossing over the statistic.

In addition, be careful not to bombard others with numbers grouped together in the same paragraph. For example:

> McCarthy Transport has a fleet of 29 buses servicing 73 cities across three states. Our team of 96 drivers and 15 customer service representatives serve an aggregate population of 543 000 people.

I'm not anti-numbers, and I'm not suggesting these figures aren't important. it's just that most people can't absorb a series of numbers in quick succession. Instead, spread out numerical data on your 'About' page so readers have the time to digest each figure and how it fits into the context of your story. If you shoot out statistics and figures machine-gun style, most readers or listeners simply won't take them in.

So what makes a good 'About' page and how do you ensure that yours hits the mark?

You want an effective 'About' page so people not only understand what your business is about but then want to do business with you. So how do you create a page that achieves this? Here's a structured approach that will ensure you cover all your bases:

Your four core points	Who? What? How? Why? When? Your point of difference
Your four supplementary points	Birth of the business Understanding your customers' struggles Customer success Achievements and credentials
Conclusion	Your call to action

Your four core points
This forms the basis of your 'About' page. Almost all businesses will benefit from featuring their four core points.

Who? What?

Identify your company and clearly explain what you do. Let's take this fictional example:

> The Gourmet Healthy Cuisine company provides nutritious organic home-delivered meals to busy professionals who love food but don't have time to cook.

How?

You've already clearly defined your target customer. Now explain how you can help them. Depending on what kind of business you run, you need to describe what happens when customers buy from you and how their lives are affected by what you offer. For example:

> We deliver an entire week of breakfasts, lunches and dinners to your door. These are all pre-packaged so all you have to do is reach into the fridge and pull out the clearly labelled meal corresponding to the day of the week. There is almost no preparation or cooking time. You just heat or assemble the items—and enjoy!

When? Why?

Reveal when you founded your company and why. For example:

> Founded in 2005 by CEO Cindy Homewood, Gourmet Healthy Cuisine was created after Cindy—a self-confessed foodie and avid home chef—had pursued a corporate career that meant working long hours but never finding time to cook, shop or eat properly. She put on weight, became depressed and searched for a solution that would allow her to balance her nutrition with her hectic lifestyle. Finding none, she knew there was a gap in the market for delicious and healthy meals that were ready to eat at a minute's notice.

Here is where you can adapt to your specific circumstances. For example, if Cindy started Gourmet Healthy Cuisine only last week, she might not want to dwell on how new the business is, particularly if she doesn't have any customers yet! Instead, focus on a different aspect of 'when'. For example:

With 10 years' experience as a nutritionist, Cindy founded Gourmet Healthy Cuisine because she realised that there were no convenient pre-packaged but highly nutritious dinner options for busy professionals.

Your point of difference

How are you different from your competitors? What is your unique selling point? You can just use generic statements like 'we have superior customer service' or 'we offer a wide range of products', but it's more effective to identify tangible points of difference that really set you apart from other businesses like yours. For example:

All Gourmet Healthy Cuisine meals are prepared using organic ingredients, hormone-free, free-range chicken and vegetables grown in our market garden, and all have been tested and approved by the Heart Foundation.

Your four supplementary points

You may want to include some or all of the four supplementary points, depending on whether you think they will add value to your story. Don't dismiss these points as optional extras. Try to work them into your 'About' page, but don't force them into your story if they don't fit naturally.

Birth of the business

There's often some romance, even intrigue, surrounding the birth of a business. Apple's Steve Jobs built a prototype computer with Steve Wozniak in his parents' garage. Ruth Handler invented the Barbie Doll when she realised her daughter preferred playing with adult-looking paper dolls. Nike founder Bill Bowerman based Nike's unique rubber sole on the pattern of the waffle iron his wife Barbara used to make their breakfast.

If there is a point of interest or intrigue, a milestone or turning point, relating to how your business started, it's worth highlighting this on your 'About' page. For example:

Cindy turned her back on a successful career as a corporate lawyer soon after she was admitted to hospital from exhaustion. It was a turning point in her life. She knew her career wasn't worth losing her health over. As soon as she got out of hospital, she resigned from her job and started Gourmet Healthy Cuisine.

For walking frame manufacturer Sue Chen, meeting Yolanda was a turning point in the way she thought about walking frames. Not all businesses need to be steeped in some kind of mythical lore. Your fallback position is the passion story you identified in the previous chapter. The point is to focus on an incident or experience, or simply an emotion or realisation, that has given the business momentum or direction. This brings your business to life and helps people understand there's a greater purpose behind it.

The key thing to remember is that every business is different. If the history of how your business came about isn't particularly interesting or inspiring, then don't feel compelled to include it.

What if you weren't around when your business was founded? Let's say you bought into it long after it was established. Then talk about why you bought into the company. What inspired you about the business that made you feel like you had to be a part of it?

Understanding your customers' struggles

As we've learned, people are intrigued by stories that involve struggles and challenges, or rather stories in which people overcome the challenges they face. I'm not suggesting that this is the place to feature a laundry list of challenges that *you* have faced in your business. Rather, this is where you show that you understand the struggles your customer may be going through. The aim is to show empathy towards your prospective customers. Whether they want to renovate their home, lose weight or create an iPhone app, you want to demonstrate that you understand the issues they are facing. Usually the best way to do this is by revealing that you've been in the same position yourself.

The 'About' page for leading hair removal business Nad's indicates that the business was created because the founder understood the everyday struggles of her customers:

> Nad's was founded in 1992 by Sue Ismiel, a mother who created an extremely effective natural, no heat, hair removal product for her young daughter from ingredients she found in her own kitchen.
>
> The use of Nad's Natural Hair Removal Gel spread from Sue Ismiel's family to friends, and in what seemed like a blink of an eye, to the entire consumer market of Australia, winning awards and dominating its category.

Nad's also builds trust and credibility in their products by emphasising that they weren't developed by lab-coated men who don't understand, and could never understand, the nuances of hair removal for women. The original product was created by a mother specifically for her daughter. The implication: it was created with love; it is not harmful; and it works.

Customer success stories

Of course, not all entrepreneurs find themselves in the same position as their customers. Cardiologists don't have to experience heart attacks in order to save lives. You don't need to commit a crime in order to be a barrister. This is where your customer success stories can play a huge part in establishing your social credentials. Customer success stories can be among the most powerful marketing tools in your arsenal. In fact, we've dedicated the next chapter to how to find these stories and where to use them.

In your 'About' page, you should make it clear what customers can expect from working with you. How will their lives change? The key here is to focus on the positive impact your business can make on their lives. You can do this by using quantifiable results:

> 85 per cent of our clients report a significant improvement in their hay fever symptoms after using Hayfever Begone.

Or through compelling testimonials:

> 'With the advice I received form Careers Coaches Unlimited, I revamped my résumé, have become more confident in the workplace and have just been offered my dream job!'

Your achievements or credentials

You might think that this is where you get to wax lyrical about your achievements or credentials. But remember, this section is not about boosting your ego with a mile-long list of every award or mark of distinction you've ever received. Focus on the ones that are going to build trust and credibility with your target market. For example, if you're a chiropractor, you should list your qualifications and any chiropractic achievements you have under your belt. However, if your website is named as a finalist in your local chamber of commerce's digital awards, that might be a nice nod to whoever designed it, but it's not going to win you too many points as a specialist in back pain.

Don't show off just for the sake of it. This is an area where people can sometimes get too broad with their definition of 'achievements'. If you list every distinction you've ever been nominated for, no matter how minor or irrelevant, you may look like you're trying too hard. And if you give the impression that you're clutching at straws, you call into question the reputation you've worked so hard to build. I once knew an audiologist who worked at centres for the profoundly deaf. In her biography and marketing materials she proudly displayed the fact that she had attended Boston University. Many people were less than impressed when they discovered she'd attended the university for a mammoth stretch of two whole weeks. Moral of the story: highlight achievements that will build trust and credibility, not call it into question.

Conclusion: Your call to action

Round off your 'About' page with a call to action. This doesn't have to be a hard sell or promo code or free set of steak knives, and it doesn't have to be complex. It should simply guide your target audience to the next step. It might be something as simple as:

> If you'd like to find out more about which healthy meal plans suit your lifestyle and budget, call us on 02 9555 1234 and we'll guide you through to the best option for your needs.

Where else can you use this?

In addition to your 'About' page, remember that you can use any of the core or supplementary points in your story in brochures, marketing materials, speeches or just general conversation with customers or prospects. The key is to take the time to identify each point so you're ready to articulate them when you feel it's the right time to drop them into the discussion.

Some prospective customers will ask you questions about your business over the phone. Yes, the phone. Remember that old-fashioned thing we used all the time before everything went online? If a customer is at the stage where they've picked up the phone to call you, chances are they've already done a bit of research into what you have to offer and may even be ready to buy. The phone call is almost a formality—to check whether you're a real business, to seek reassurance they're dealing with nice people, and to clarify any questions they may have about your product or service. However, while *you* may know your business story inside out, what happens if you're not the one to answer the phone? Have you equipped your team with the tools they need to tell your business story effectively? Give them a cheat sheet. It might look something like this:

Your four core points	
Who? What?	The Gourmet Healthy Cuisine company provides nutritious organic home-delivered meals to busy professionals who love food but don't have time to cook.
How?	We deliver an entire week of breakfasts, lunches and dinners to your door. These are all pre-packaged so all you have to do is reach into the fridge and pull out the clearly labelled meal corresponding to the day of the week. There is almost no preparation or cooking time. All you have to do to is heat or assemble the items—and enjoy!
Why? When?	Founded in 2005 by CEO Cindy Homewood, Gourmet Healthy Cuisine was created after Cindy—a self-confessed foodie and avid home chef—had pursued a corporate career that meant working long hours but never finding time to cook, shop or eat properly. She put on weight, became depressed and searched for a solution that would allow her to balance her nutrition with her hectic lifestyle. Finding none, she knew there was a gap in the market for delicious and healthy meals that were ready to eat at a minute's notice.

Your point of difference	All Gourmet Healthy Cuisine meals are prepared using organic ingredients, hormone-free, free-range chicken and vegetables grown in our market garden, and all have been tested and approved by the Heart Foundation.
Your four supplementary points	
Birth of the business	Cindy turned her back on a successful career as a corporate lawyer soon after she was admitted to hospital from exhaustion. That was a turning point in her life. She knew her career wasn't worth losing her health over. As soon as she got out of hospital, she resigned from her job and started Gourmet Healthy Cuisine.
Understanding your customers' struggles	We know how hectic your lifestyle can be. You're juggling work, children, errands and family commitments, with barely enough time to breathe, let alone shop for groceries and cook. We want to make life easier for you so you have more time to spend on the things that are important to you.
Customer success stories	87 per cent of people who try our service end up becoming long-term clients. 'Gourmet Healthy Cuisine is so easy. An entire week's worth of meals arrives at our door every Monday. My stress levels have gone down, I'm eating healthier and I've even lost two kilos.'—Anna Margolies
Achievements and credentials	Every menu is created by a nutritionist and all meals are prepared by five-star chefs.
Conclusion	
Your call to action	Would you like to place an order now?

You can download a template from the exclusive resources section at <www.powerstoriesbook.com> so you can create your own cheat sheet.

Never underestimate the power of your call to action

When I first started my business, I was the one answering the phones and responding to queries about the writing courses offered at the Sydney Writers' Centre. I'd tell people all about the Centre, listen to their dreams about getting published and suggest the course most suited to fulfilling their goals. They'd ask me lots of questions about the topics covered in the course, the kinds of assignments they might have and what types of students typically enrolled. I'd happily oblige, and when I'd answered all their queries I'd always end with: 'Well, why you don't think about it and if you have any other questions, just give me a call back and I'd be happy to help.'

I didn't want to be pushy. I had a romantic notion that the courses would speak for themselves. After doing this for about eight months and making a respectable but modest income, I decided to experiment with a different approach. I changed by parting message to: 'Would you like to enrol?' Nine times of out of ten, they simply said, 'Yes.'

With that simple call to action, I had converted a prospective customer into a paying one. The reality was that they had all the information they needed and they were ready to buy. I just needed to give them the opportunity to do so.

Do you have a call to action? If you're not at the coalface dealing with queries, have you equipped your team with the right words and phrases so they can put forward a call to action to your prospective customers?

Your actions

Your business story
Imagine your ideal customer is meeting you for the first time. Perhaps you meet at a networking event, or they stumble across your website while browsing the internet. You have a small window in which to pique their interest in your business. Use the time frames suggested below as a practical guideline. If you exceed the time limits, you'll need to be more succinct. Follow these steps or download your Business Story template in the exclusive resources section at <www.powerstoriesbook.com>.

1 Create your 10-second elevator speech.
2 Create your 30-second pitch.
3 Write your 'About' page (or review your existing one) based on the guideline in this chapter.
4 Distribute the above to any staff who may need to use this information.

CHAPTER 5
Your customer story

An Angry Bird plush toy sits on Mark Hayes' office desk. Next to it is a temporary tattoo transfer, a dodocase iPad cover and a row of Tabasco sauce bottles. No, Mark isn't an oddball collector, he's the director of marketing and public relations at Shopify, an ecommerce platform that helps entrepreneurs create their own online stores. In his office in Ottawa, other desks are strewn with an equally eclectic mix of products that include bagless tea, colourful socks and a vintage poster. They are all products sold by different businesses that use Shopify as their ecommerce platform.

It looks like Mark has his job cut out for him. He's marketing a complex technology to businesses of all sizes in a broad range of industries. After all, his target customer is … anyone who wants to create an online store. With such a broad brief, it can be hard to develop a targeted marketing campaign. But there is one message that all business owners understand—the Entrepreneur's Journey.

So rather than dwelling on all the technological features that make up the back end of the Shopify system, Mark and his team have developed Shopify Stories, an online mini-series of stories about their customers. 'The stories tell the tales of interesting Shopify store owners—how they started their businesses, why they decided to sell online and how it's changed their lives,' says Mark.

Mark is using one of the most effective power stories of all—the Customer Story.

One of these customers is 25-year-old Sophie Kovic. Before Sophie discovered Shopify she was earning a modest income working part-time as a manager and projectionist at a cinema in the small coastal town of Byron Bay in the far north of New South Wales in Australia.

Her boyfriend, Timothy Butterfield, owned a cafe that was struggling through tough economic times. Timothy had developed a repetitive strain injury in his wrist but was forced to work long hours to survive financially. It was 2011, Sophie was a new mother and the couple realised they had to take drastic action if they were going to make ends meet. To meet their mortgage payments, they rented out rooms in their house. 'It was like a boarding house,' says Sophie. 'We had people living in our house on and off for two years.'

But it still wasn't enough. 'We worked as much as we both could, taking shifts with Archie, who was our newborn,' says Sophie. 'But we ended up losing the house anyway. It was all so upsetting and very rough. But it gave us a chance at a fresh start.'

Sophie knew she wanted a better life. 'I was sick of always worrying about money and I had always wanted to start a business,' she says. 'At the time, I read *The 4-Hour Work Week* by Tim Ferriss.'

Part of the premise of *The 4-Hour Work Week* is to create a business that generates passive income so you can pursue other goals, whether that's spending time with your family, travelling or starting another business. Following Ferriss's advice, Sophie searched Google Insights for products with a ratio of high interest and low competition—and discovered feathered hair extensions. These hair accessories are woven into hair and feature the kind of feathers often used as lures in fly-fishing.

'I already had an interest in human hair extensions, and when I was searching for those key words, 'feather' kept popping up. When I did more research I realised that about 30 000 people were searching for feathered hair extensions each month but that there were only two people selling them online. At the time, I didn't really even know what they were. But I found out, and went from there.'

It wasn't long before Sophie's house was full of feathers. 'There were feathers everywhere,' she says. Sales flowed in immediately and, with help from backpacker workers and an assistant, her online store was born. Sophie primarily used Google Adwords to attract people to her site and supplemented this marketing by promoting her products via her blog and social media. At the height of its popularity in mid 2011, she turned over $100 000 in a single a month.

'I banked more in the first few months than I ever dreamed of making,' says Sophie, who has now expanded her range to include human hair extensions. 'I wish I had discovered it just a couple of months before. Then we wouldn't have lost our house, because we only needed $40 000 to make up the gap to give the bank. But at the time we didn't have that money.'

After two months in business, Sophie decided to outsource the administration, packing and sending functions to her assistant, who works from her own home, just down the road from Sophie. Even after these costs, she's sitting pretty. Now she has a clear system in place, Sophie works less than an hour a week on her business.

'I decided that I wanted to sell online because it's easy and low-cost to get started. There are also so few recurring costs. No rent, no utilities and no staff to begin with. Traditional retail is looking very hard these days.'

Sophie's hair extensions sell to individuals and hairdressers, and she is looking towards expanding into other products in the future. 'While the feather business has given me a full-time income, including enough money to fund a four-month holiday in Thailand for my family in 2011, I still work part time as a manager/projectionist at the Dendy Cinema in Byron Bay.

'My decision to stay working there while paying someone to run my business full time may seem strange, but the actual day-to-day work in running an online business selling feathers isn't that stimulating. This way I can still enjoy my work at the cinema part time, develop new business ideas and be with my baby boy.'

Why is your customer story so useful?

A summarised version of Sophie's story appears among Shopify's success stories. Mark Hayes sees these stories as far more engaging than any list of the platform's features and benefits. 'You don't convert people with the technology. You convert them by showing them what the technology can do,' he says. 'There's still this idea that selling online is difficult. It's not—at all. If you have 15 minutes and you can use email, you can build a fully functional, beautiful online store that's open 24 hours a day, 365 days a year, and sells all around the world.'

In your customer story, you get to cast your customer in the role of the hero in their very own story, just as Mark Hayes has done with Shopify's customers. Of course your customers may not be business owners like Sophie; they won't necessarily be on the Entrepreneur's Journey. Maybe their goal is to lose weight, or to get a good night's sleep, or to repair their relationship with their spouse, or to renovate their home, or even to own a luxury yacht so they can sail around the Greek Islands. Chances are, they're on a quest, and that could involve a material goal (like the yacht) or an emotional one (like saving their marriage).

Your customer's journey is one of the most powerful stories in your arsenal. However, this isn't about one story of a single customer. It's about building up a range of stories from many different customers, because it's these stories that often have the biggest impact in convincing and converting your prospects. Here's why.

There are four key outcomes when you highlight an effective customer story. They are as follows:

- *You prove that your business provides results.* You need to paint a picture of the impact your business has had on your customer. 'Before' and 'after' photos are the classic example of this.
- *You show that you have helped people 'just like them'.* Your customer stories help people understand the type of people you work with. More important, they demonstrate to your prospects that you have helped people 'just like them'.
- *You establish credibility.* While the hero in this story is your customer, remember to cast yourself (or your business) as one of the characters—that is, someone who plays a key role in helping the customer achieve their goal.
- *You're endorsed by a third party.* Your customer story is an implicit endorsement from that customer. It's not just you waxing lyrical about how great you are. You have evidence that *other people* think you're pretty darn good, too!

So how and where can you use these stories?

There are two main types of stories: those generated and shared by your customer, and those generated and shared by you.

Stories generated and shared by your customer

Some customer stories will be initiated by your customer. These include:

- reviews on online review sites such as Yelp.com, online store reviews, restaurant review sites, and so on
- reviews on personal blogs, Twitter, Facebook and other social media
- word of mouth.

In the old days, before social sharing sites, our customers shared their stories with their friends at barbecues or Friday night drinks or waiting at the school gates. These days a customer can tweet about a fantastic (or horrendous) experience on their smartphone in a matter of seconds. They may not have even left the store and their comments on your product or service are already being broadcast to hundreds, if not thousands, of their followers. And, depending on their sphere of influence, these comments could soon be retweeted, forwarded or shared even further by their friends.

This is great if they have raved about your business. If that's the case, then you *want* them to be the spark that spreads a fire of positive comments about you. To increase your chances of this happening, you simply need to deliver fantastic service or a quality product. You want to give them every reason in the world to share an amazing story about you. Let them take care of the rest. If their comments are negative, though, you need to get into damage control mode—fast. You need to shape the ending to their story.

Stories generated and shared by you

While the stories generated by your customers will largely depend on their (hopefully positive) experience with you, it pays to be proactive when it comes to the customer stories that are within your control. These are the ones that are found, packaged and shared by you—with permission from your customer, of course. They include the following:

- Customer testimonials you can feature on your website and in brochures and other marketing materials. These are typically brief comments provided by your customer.
- Case studies, which are usually longer stories—often up to a page—that go into more detail about your customer's journey with you. Apart from featuring these on your website, you might use them in a more comprehensive marketing document such as a written tender or proposal to a client.

In addition to running my own business, I also mentor small business owners. I often talk about how important their customer testimonials are. These business owners nod their heads in agreement, tell me they understand how powerful these testimonials can be in converting new customers, and assure me they'll feature some on their website ASAP. The next time we meet for a mentoring session, I check out their websites and marketing materials. No customer stories. No testimonials. When I ask why, the reason is almost always the same: 'No one has given any to me yet.'

Oh. My. Goodness. The customer testimonial fairy isn't going to drop them into your lap on a silver platter. Customers aren't magically going to whip up a succinct paragraph about how much they love you and email it to you apropos of nothing. You need to ask them.

Of course, that's when I hear some people say, 'Oh but I couldn't ask.' To which I respond, 'Why the hell not?'

The key is that you don't sit there and wait for a customer to tell you how good you are. You need to seek out these stories in a systematic way. The key word here is 'systematic'. If you don't build this into a regular workflow pattern, then it's going to be one of those jobs that falls by the wayside, something the occasional intern will compile, only for it to be forgotten until the next one comes along.

At the Sydney Writers' Centre, we share at least one of our customer stories *every week* because we have a policy that our weekly e-newsletter always features a 'student success'. That's our equivalent of a customer story. If we didn't have a system for finding, packaging and sharing these stories, we'd be in a mad panic every week trying to find a customer story to share with our community.

If you don't have a system to identify, package and share your customer stories, you can use the following system as a guide, adapting it to suit your business. The most important thing is to *implement it* so you can start identifying valuable customer stories right now.

Finding your customer stories

You may have no shortage of wonderful customer stories. But if they are all anecdotal, or merely in the form of casual comments from appreciative customers, it can be hard to compile these stories into a powerful vehicle to grow your business. What you need is ... a system.

How to capture the data

For this to work, you need a simple and effective way to capture data. You can hand your customer a hardcopy feedback form to fill out, or you can do it electronically by emailing them a link to an online form or survey.

So which one should you choose? Quite simply, the one that most customers will use. I have a strong preference for capturing data electronically. This way there is no need for someone to input the data into a spreadsheet or other online format. All the responses are captured in one place, and you can search for names or keywords in seconds instead of taking forever to flip through hundreds of sheets of paper. However, if you don't have much success with getting your customers to provide feedback online, you may have to go the hardcopy route.

Whichever you choose, make sure it happens like clockwork. Embed it in your workflow processes. For example, if you're a health practitioner, make sure you ask for feedback at the end of every session or series of sessions. If you're a marketing consultancy, identify a triggering incident that will ensure you seek your customer's feedback at the ideal time. You might even automate it. For example, your workflow system might be set up so that whenever a final invoice is issued to a customer, the feedback form is sent two days later.

Obviously, you will need to determine the ideal time to ask for feedback. You want to ensure that you're asking for feedback after the job or project is complete so your customer can comment on whether or not you've achieved the brief and met their expectations.

If you've sold a product, you need to give your customer enough time to use it before reviewing it, but you don't want to leave it so long that their experience with you has become a distant memory.

What data do you need?

I've seen too many feedback forms that simply ask: 'Tell us what you think of us.' While this might elicit some responses, it's too vague and broad to be of any real use. You want to be able to use these responses on your website or in marketing materials in a powerful way.

This is powerful:

> 'The best part of ABC Gym is John. He's helped me understand nutrition in a whole new light. I'm stronger than I've ever been, I no longer have back pain and I quit smoking. This gym is a great place for people who are serious about getting fitter but who don't want to work out with meatheads.'

This is not:

> 'Great gym!'

The latter may be a nice comment from a satisfied customer but it's not a story. You need to encourage responses that turn into powerful stories, and you do *that* by asking the right questions. Here are some questions that could be used by any type of business. But you should consider additional questions specific to your customers or industry.

What has been the best part of your experience?

This typically results in a positive comment. But the simple fact that you are asking your customer to describe 'the best' part of their experience often results in a response that is powerful enough to become the entire testimonial.

What areas can we improve on?

This is a great opportunity to listen to your customers and learn where you can improve. You probably won't use it in your customer story, but it shows your customer that you are serious about hearing the good and the bad.

Would you recommend us to your friends?

Hopefully, they say yes!

If yes, what would you say?

These answers are most valuable because customers are talking about your business as a whole. Rather than commenting on the specific product or service they've just bought or experienced, they are describing their overall experience with your brand.

Can we use your comments in our marketing materials?

Always remember to ask this. You don't want to collate the most wonderful comments and recommendations, only to find you don't actually have permission to use them. Remember that some people are very particular about their privacy and, for a multitude of reasons, may not want you to use their name and testimonial. You need to respect that. Always ask for permission. I suggest you simply provide check boxes for the answers:

> Can we use your comments on our marketing materials?
> ☐ Yes
> ☐ No

That way, people can simply tick their response. In my experience, when you leave the question open-ended, you have a higher incidence of people leaving it unanswered.

Increasing the response rate from customers

If you're not getting many responses when you ask for feedback, it's time to tweak your system.

The ask

Do you need to craft your 'ask' so it encourages more feedback from customers? Change the message until you start getting a better response. This 'ask' might be fine:

> We would be most grateful if you could give us your feedback on your experience with us. Please do this by clicking on <u>this link</u>.

But the following might generate a better response:

> Thank you for choosing to do business with us. We're constantly looking at ways to improve our services and would love your feedback on your recent experience. We want to ensure we're providing services that suit your needs, so if you have time to complete our one-minute survey, we'd really appreciate it. You can do <u>that here</u>.

The mechanics

Are you making it easy for customers to provide their feedback. If they have to click through a complicated series of links, they may give up. When I first started out, I sent questions via email. These days I use Survey Monkey to send online surveys to my community. It's straightforward and very easy for customers to use. If you want to sample a quick survey, visit the exclusive resources section at <www.powerstoriesbook.com>.

The key is to make it simple. You don't want your customers to have to log into special forums or jump through hoops in order to give you feedback.

The questions

Have you included too many questions in your feedback survey? If a busy customer sees a raft of questions, they are less inclined to respond. It might be tempting to use this as a sneaky form of market research for your other products or services as well, but if you load your survey with too many questions about other areas of your business, you're taking the focus away from the point of the exercise.

Keep your questions succinct, focused and designed to extract a powerful customer testimonial you can use.

Review your data and extract customer stories

Depending on how frequently you ask for feedback, you should schedule regular times to review the responses. This may be daily, weekly or monthly, depending on the nature of your business and the volume of responses.

If you're just starting out in business, you're the one who's likely to be reviewing the responses. At this stage it can be one of the most valuable activities you do, helping you to catch any potential problems or issues early. Even negative customer feedback can be a godsend, because it raises red flags so you can address issues before they become full-blown problems.

Reviewing your customers' responses can also provide you with valuable clues as to the next step in their journey. In the early days of the Sydney Writers' Centre, we provided only a small number of writing courses, but as we reviewed the feedback from our customers we took note of the types of courses and services our students told us they wanted. That helped us determine which courses to offer next without worrying about demand—we knew the demand was there!

Share your customer stories

Once you've extracted a series of powerful customer stories, you need a systematic way to use them. There's no point in having a pile of wonderful testimonials just sitting in a document. You want to share them (providing your customers have given their permission, of course). There are two main ways to share these stories:

Externally

You need to feature your customer testimonials so your prospects can read them, so think about the pages on your website they visit most often. If your leads are generated when people download a free report from your site, it may be worthwhile including some powerful testimonials in that free report.

Every business is different, so you need to determine the best place to feature your customer testimonials. Can you feature a customer story in your e-newsletter? Or on a dedicated page on your website? Or maybe next to a specific product in your online store or on your blog? The key here is to *use* this testimonial. If you don't, you're wasting an opportunity to showcase the impact you have on your customers' lives. The best way to do this is to adopt a structured approach. For example:

Week 1: Feature a customer testimonial in your email newsletter.
Week 2: Feature a longer case study about a customer story on your blog.
Week 3: Highlight a customer success story on Facebook or LinkedIn.

When reviewing your survey data, you may find that certain stories stand out. Maybe working with you has had such a life-changing effect on one of your customers that you want to shout it from the rooftops. Running a short testimonial taken from the handful of sentences your customer provided via the survey may not do it justice. If this is the case, contact the customer to get more detail to tell a bigger story. Sophie Kovic, with her feathered hair extensions, is a great example of this. These sorts of case studies not only are valuable to showcase as blog posts but can also be used in brochures, proposals and other marketing documents.

Internally

Remember to share your stories within your team too. Not all team members will be at the coalface dealing with customers. Those in operations, logistics or accounts may not get much exposure to how their efforts in the business ultimately affect customers. Sharing these stories with your team puts their work into context and shows them they are part of a bigger picture.

Mark Hayes sees these stories as offering an inspiring reminder to the Shopify team. Rather than focusing on bringing in as many customers as possible, the stories remind the team of the human faces at the other end of their admin dashboard. 'Shopify Stories validates what we do here: we help people. We don't just come into the office and work nine to five to bring in as many customers as possible. What we do here makes a huge difference in people's lives. We've helped create millionaires, we've helped bring single mothers out of poverty, we've helped make people famous. It helps instil a sense of pride in our staff.'

Video testimonials

Although customer testimonials in written form are currently perfectly fine, it won't be long before video testimonials will become de rigueur. They've already crept into many sites—mine included—but I expect they will become even more popular in the next few years.

Consumers will move beyond wanting to read customer reviews; they will want to see those customers. Before long it will become perfectly normal to record a video of yourself doing a quick review of a restaurant or other consumer experience. iPhone applications that record and store 15-second video soundbites (for example, Tout. com and Viddly.com) are already gaining popularity. People may get used to the 15-second video soundbite as quickly as they got used to the 140-character status update on Twitter. The day hasn't come yet when it's vital for every business owner to feature video testimonials from customers, but it's not far off.

Good old-fashioned conversation

While we've dwelt a lot on sharing your customer stories electronically, it's vital to remember to use them in good old-fashioned conversation too. Give your marketing and customer service team—or anyone who liaises with prospects—access to the data you've collected on your customer stories, so they can draw on this pool of stories when talking to potential customers.

Sometimes, telling a prospect a story about how another customer has benefited from your product or service is just the thing you need to seal the deal. You don't have to use these stories in any kind of hard sell. But you need to know them in order to showcase how you help people, particularly if your service offering is esoteric, complex or homogenous.

Create a community for your customers

When you create a community for your customers, they end up telling one another their stories. This confirms and validates their experience with you. If they share positive experiences, this strengthens your brand, because they recognise that their experience with you was not a one-off, that in fact it happens all the time. It's about cross-pollinating your customer stories, which in turn builds loyalty.

It's also a marketing machine on steroids. Your most valuable customers are the people who have bought from you before. They have already got to know, like and trust you, so it's easier to convince them to buy from you again than to woo a complete stranger.

When your customers talk to each other, they often compare notes about the specific products and services they've purchased. This is where the power of building a community kicks in, because they are doing your marketing for you. Without your sending out any promotional emails or brochures, the people in your 'tribe' or community are already talking about your products or services.

I recently spoke at a conference run by Etsy.com about how to use networking and social media to build your profile and boost your business. Etsy is an online marketplace dominated by those selling handmade or vintage items. Its users come from all over the world, and most know each other only via their online profiles. These conferences are a way for like-minded people in this community (they all have online stores on Etsy, and they're all crafty) to meet in real life. This connection 'in real life' forges relationships and builds a stronger community after they return to their craft studios, sewing rooms and workbenches.

Your customers' stories are so much more than just testimonials on your website. They are power stories that can resonate with prospects—convince, convert and connect you to a customer for life.

Your actions

Your customer stories
Stop. Pull yourself away from your daily grind. Think about people, real people, customers you actually know. Picture their faces, write down their names and think about the impact your products or services have had on their lives. Think about the types of customer stories that truly showcase what you do.

1 Download your Customer Story template in the exclusive resources section at <www.powerstoriesbook.com>.
2 Determine a systematic and efficient way to collect stories from your customers. This might be via an electronic or hardcopy feedback form.

3 Implement step 2. That's right—take action! This is where most entrepreneurs fall down. Don't get stuck on this step. Move forward.
4 Schedule regular times to review the data and extract the best stories.
5 Consider if there are specific places (such as your website or newsletter) where the stories should be featured.
6 Make a point of sharing key stories with your team so they can see the difference they are making to customers. For example, this could be a regular item on the agenda at team meetings.
7 Foster an online community where your customers can interact, get to know one another and build loyalty to your brand.

CHAPTER 6

Your pitch story

In Mick Liubinskas's office there's no shortage of ideas. As co-founder of Australian web business incubator Pollenizer, Mick hears countless pitches each week from aspiring web entrepreneurs who all want to be the next Mark Zuckerberg or Larry Page. These pitches come in via his website, when he is cornered at start-up networking events, and through a myriad emails and phone calls from start-up-founder wannabes who just want half an hour of his time to sell him on what they're convinced is going to be the Next Big Thing.

Mick says working in the world of start-ups is like the dating scene. There's the approach (where you sidle up to someone at a bar), the introduction, and a bit of flirting before you establish if you want to get to know each other. 'When you meet someone in a bar, you don't launch straight into your life story,' says Mick. 'You need to capture someone's attention first, so that means you have to nail your elevator pitch.'

In chapter 4 we talked about how you should craft your elevator pitch. But when your business is nothing more than an idea, you need a slightly different kind of pitch, because you haven't exactly got a lot to work with. No track record, no customers and, in some cases, no real business yet! Perhaps you had a brainwave in the shower and think you have the idea for the next Instagram. Or while you were walking the dog you suffered an entrepreneurial seizure that has your mind buzzing with the conviction that your idea is going to be bigger than eBay.

Before you can turn this into a fully fledged business, you have to convince everyone from investors and customers to suppliers and eventually employees that you have a viable product. That's what your Pitch Story is all about.

It's this pitch that will help your idea begin to take shape. For Mick and co-founder Phil Morle, it's a story the entrepreneurs they work with have to get right. In an office in inner-city Surry Hills in Sydney, Pollenizer team members are clustered in 'pods', with each pod working a single start-up with the co-founder. Mick says they typically invest in non-technical entrepreneurs to launch online businesses. Mick has long experience in the start-up space, including two years as chief marketing officer for file-sharing service Kazaa, best known for peer-to-peer sharing of MP3 files.

Pollenizer has some similarities to the US web incubator YCombinator, headed by tech luminary Paul Graham, which provides initial seed capital and intensive coaching through its highly competitive 13-week boot camps before attracting other, longer term investors. The key difference is that Pollenizer is much more 'high touch', operating as a true co-founder with the entrepreneur. Pollenizer takes equity in the start-up and guides it from inception and development to growth and exit. Since it was founded in 2008, it has received thousands of pitches, worked with over 200 companies and incorporated more than 30 of them.

Pollenizer's investments include social payments platform Pygg, online coaching site Coachy.com and employee recognition application Wooboard.com. It made headlines in January 2011 when it sold its most successful start-up, Spreets, to Yahoo!7 for a reported $40 million.

Intrigue, don't scare off

Just like the dating scene, your pitch needs to intrigue someone enough that they want to talk to you, but not be so wacky that it scares them off. 'If someone tells me that they're going to beat

Facebook and make a billion dollars in the first 12 months, I stop listening,' says Mick. 'But the opposite is also true. If someone says they're going to "try to crack the market", then it's too weak.'

'It can be a tough balance, because you need to be exciting enough to get my attention but not crazy enough that I think you're a nut bag.'

Your Pitch Story is an important power story in your arsenal. This applies even if your business or product has nothing to do with the web. You need to master the pitch for any idea that's new. If you're explaining the concept of a traditional business—say, a doctor's surgery, a childcare centre or a car hire company—these are typically concepts that consumers are familiar with. It can be harder to convince people of a new idea, however, especially if it's something that hasn't been done before. In the world of web-based start-ups, sometimes the technology is not the biggest barrier. In fact, it's often the least of your problems. If you don't effectively communicate what that technology can *do* and how it will be embraced by users, this is where you'll stall. Not because you don't have a good idea, but because you don't explain it in a way that resonates with people.

So what are the essential elements of a pitch story? When you're trying to convince investors to part with their hard-earned cash and invest in a brand-new idea, Mick says, your pitch story needs to be clear on two things: that your idea solves a problem and that you have the tenacity and passion to make it happen.

How does your idea solve a problem?

You need to show that there's a market for your product and you do this by showing that your idea can solve a widespread problem. After all, you don't have any sales projections because you haven't taken the product to market yet. You can't rely on historical industry data because no-one has done this before. It's so new that there aren't even any meaningful industry benchmarks to compare it to.

So what can you do? Well, words alone aren't going to cut it. Especially not if you're asking someone to fund your Big Idea. Then again, an endless series of Excel spreadsheets filled with projected cash flow figures won't necessarily get you over the line either. Anyone can fill up a spreadsheet with numbers, but numbers alone won't do the convincing. The key is to show that those numbers are achievable. And that boils down to convincing people that there is demand for your product.

This is where you need to take action in order to create the story you need. That's right. You need to play an active part in moving your story forward so you have a pitch story worth listening to. You need to be the author of your very own choose-your-own-adventure novel, and to make your story compelling enough that the other characters want to come on the journey with you.

The best action step to take is to do whatever you need to show that people—that is, people other than friends and family—will buy your product. Eric Reis, in his book *The Lean Startup*, refers to creating a 'minimum viable product'. That's exactly what Mick did with Coachy.com, a site where you can book one-on-one video coaching with experts ranging from guitar teachers and chefs to surf instructors. It's an online business co-founded by Pollenizer and entrepreneur Luke Grana.

'We launched the business within 24 hours of having the idea,' says Mick. By that, Mick means they created a minimum viable product to see if anyone would use the service. They didn't build an entire website. They didn't spend big on advertising. They didn't invest years in research and development.

'We faked it,' says Mick.

They used a single-page website to explain the concept, tweeted about it and within two hours had their first sale. Instead of coaching the customer via a not-yet-built online portal, they simply used Skype video. A series of disparate platforms—for booking, paying, scheduling and video—were used to simulate what Coachy.com would ultimately provide through one interface. These early tests of its minimum viable product enabled the founders to bring depth and anecdotal evidence to their pitch story.

Identify investor empathy

Apart from demonstrating the commercial demand for your idea, your story needs to be tailored to each investor—or to whoever you are pitching to, for that matter. It also needs to be tailored to each investor's interests and motivations. It's not always about dollars and cents, Mick says. 'The stronger the empathy that the investor has with the ideas, the higher the chance you have to succeed.'

'I call it "blood on the floor". If something is not bleeding with such a strong pain, then the investor will think that it's nice to solve but it's not necessarily a product they need to have. The level of empathy to the size of the pain is the leverage you have to close the deal.'

Identifying this empathy relies on two things: *research* and *listening*. Do your research before your meeting. Find out if the person you are pitching to loves golf, hates the Liberal Party, is obsessed with AFL or has a passion for helping rescue dogs. You can glean useful information from their profile on LinkedIn, media articles and social media updates. I'm not suggesting that you throw 'Tiger Woods', 'shameful embarrassment', 'Brownlow contender' and 'cute puppy' into the same sentence. But the more research you do beforehand, the more you'll be able to tailor your stories when you are in conversation.

While it can be tempting—and nerve-racking—to pitch, it's important to remember that this shouldn't be a monologue. Listen to who you're pitching to and adjust your message as you go along. Investors will have different motivations for wanting to invest. Mick points out that some investors are not primarily driven by making huge returns on their investment. Of course they won't knock back a share of the profits if you make it big, but they may have different priorities. 'Some investors are already financially set,' says Mick. 'What they want is a journey and an experience. Sure, they hope they get their money back. But you need to shape your story so they can clearly see how they might play a role.'

Demonstrating tenacity and passion

Why are you excited about the project? What's going to keep you working till the wee hours of the morning when all the chips are down? What motivates you and how does that fit into the bigger picture? In short, tell them the story of why you're prepared to go to hell and back to make your idea work.

You need to show evidence of tenacity. Mick says: 'A good investor knows that the solution will change many times. Once you show that there is a problem worth solving, or a pain worth addressing, then you need to show you have the tenacity to solve it. To do this you need to demonstrate that you have a track record of building businesses. Because this kind of experience will make investors take a second look at you.'

If you haven't built any businesses before, then this is where evidence of your passion and persistence should kick in. 'You need to really *want* to tell me your story,' says Mick. 'Because demonstrating your passion can help compensate, in part, for lack of a track record. When complete strangers contact me wanting to have a chat about their new idea, I typically don't have time to see them. But if they email me three or four times then sometimes I do. I don't mean for that to sound arrogant but, as an investor, I need to know that they really want it.'

Open innovating and story sharing

If you think you have the coolest new business idea in the world, you want it to remain a secret before you launch it on an unsuspecting world, right? After all, you want to keep your idea totally under wraps so other people don't take it, implement it and make a motza from your light bulb moment before you've even had a chance to register your domain name.

Mick says the opposite it true. 'Don't go into stealth mode,' he says. 'Instead, share your story. In Australia in particular, we have an inventor mentality that is nowhere near as prevalent as in places like the US. In other words, we think that the "invention" is everything—and we keep it confidential. But, in fact, collaboration and "open innovation", an approach more likely to be adopted in the US, results in a better product because many people contribute ideas to improving it. That's why you can't hold back your idea and get non-disclosure agreements. This doesn't work in the early stage of a business.'

There's more to being successful in business than a great idea. A lot of people have great ideas. Far fewer people have the skills, desire or determination to execute those ideas. 'When you adopt an inventor mentality, you think that the idea is everything. In reality, it's the execution that is absolutely everything.'

In the early stages of business, Mick says, you need to share your stories as often as possible in order to do the following:

- *Obtain and react to feedback on your idea.* It's invaluable to get feedback on your idea as soon as possible. You should do this before you mortgage your family home to develop your business, only to discover that it won't actually work. This feedback might include suggestions of other people you should talk to, or alert you to other products in a similar space.

- *Refine the way you tell your story.* Tell your story multiple times to as many different people as possible. It's simply good practice and will help you determine the messages that work and that get other people excited. It will also reveal the messages that fall flat.

More than one pitch story

While most start-up pitch stories are directed at investors, Mick points out that you're actually pitching all the time. These micro-pitches have to be tailored to the priorities and expectations of the person you're talking to.

'Investors may want to hear about revenue projections, but customers don't care if you make a profit. They want to know that your product will help them or that you have great customer service. You have to pitch to your wife as well. She wants to know you can pay the rent next month. Your employees need to know they've made the right decision in joining your fledgling start-up instead of going with the security of an established company.'

Focus on one key message as your overall story, but adapt it depending on whom you're pitching to.

The 100 coffees rule

Mick advises all start-up founders to have 100 cups of coffee. This isn't an evil plot to get them addicted to caffeine. It's about giving them 100 opportunities to share their story. 'The first 20 times you tell your story, most people will ignore you,' says Mick. 'By the time you've told your story 50 times, it's much stronger. That's because, by then, you've been faced with every objection you'll come across and you'll have worked out how to overcome those objections, either by refining your product or business idea, or by telling your story in a better way.

'If you don't do this, and the first time you really tell your story is in a formal PowerPoint presentation to a room full of investors, then you've missed out on the 100 little bits of feedback that can make all the difference.'

The story you end up with is possibly unrecognisable compared with the one with which you started. With each iteration, your story—and your product—improves. This story of iteration has contributed to the success of Steve Sammartino's start-up Rentoid. com. Best explained as eBay for renting, it's a website where you can rent anything, ranging from handbags and musical instruments to jukeboxes and jet boats. People pay a small fee to list items to rent at an agreed price, while renters pay a hire fee directly to the owner of the item. (Steve is also the blogger behind the popular Startup Blog <startupblog.wordpress.com>.)

Founded in early 2007, Rentoid.com was cash-flow positive before the end of that year. This was in stark contrast to Steve's previous start-up, an anti-stress drink he launched in 2005 that not only didn't make money but cost Steve his house.

'I had a long-term launch mentality with the anti-stress drink,' says Steve. 'I wanted to fund things in the traditional way. I got venture capital investment and I wanted to make sure everything was perfect before I launched. Although I shared ideas, I always wanted to keep one or two up my sleeve. I realised it was an old-style approach that just isn't effective in today's world when there are far more nimble approaches to a start-up.' Steve began working on the business in 2005, spent that entire year building the business and launched it in early 2006. 'I was out of business before the end of 2006,' he says. 'I ended up living with my parents.'

Steve decided to take a very different approach with Rentoid.com. This was partly because he didn't invest a truckload of money to start the business. 'This time around, I decided to have an iteration mentality. I wanted to share the idea and get it out there as early as I could. I realised that was more important than getting it perfect. You share your story, get people's attention, get their feedback—and then you can iterate and improve.'

Steve also decided against angel or venture capital funding. 'I used to blog about how to find new factors of production that were democratised and cheap. I realised that I had to do what I was actually talking about. I had to embrace that story,' says Steve, who then launched for less then $1000 using a developer in Moldova he found on elance.com. In contrast to the year-long development of Steve's previous business, Rentoid.com was launched within 30 days of conception. He has used his blog at every step of his journey, sharing his ideas and plans, and the successes and failures of his business.

Steve believes this is particularly useful in today's business environment, especially if you are creating a business that may be a new concept for people. 'I think in the old world we used to tell stories of how we got here,' he says. 'In the new world we're trying to tell stories of what the future looks like. That's what smart start-ups do—they tell a story of what they want the world to look like.'

This way you can paint a vision of how customers might use your product. Ten years ago, an online portal for renting everything from photocopiers to Ferraris was unheard of. So was an app that would enable you to 'check in' to venues via your smartphone and get points that you could redeem for drinks or discounts. And back then who would have thought that you could work remotely, with your team spread across continents, by sharing files in Google Apps and communicating via Skype?

When you're at the frontier of anything, you're not only dealing with new territory but introducing the new land to everyone else. 'You need to let these people—your customers—become part of your story,' says Steve. 'You need to let them help shape the future.'

Your customers aren't the only ones to help shape your future. Steve is an ideal example of the concept that you need to *create your own story*. For example, if you don't have an amazing angle for the media, generate one. If you don't have a compelling customer testimonial, create a situation where your customer is so happy with your service that they can't help but rave about you. If you need more demand for your product so you can tell others a story about how your product works, invent demand.

That doesn't mean you should fabricate it. Not at all. When Rentoid.com first started, it suffered from a classic chicken and egg scenario: 'People couldn't rent items from the site unless others were willing to put their items up for rent,' he says. 'Conversely, some didn't want to list items unless there were clearly customers ready and willing to rent their item.' To overcome this and get the traction he needed, Steve 'invented demand'.

'I would rent things from people who had listed items to rent on the site,' he says. 'Even if I didn't actually want to rent them, I would personally go to meet them, rent the sewing machine, put it in my house for the weekend and then bring it back, because I knew that once they experienced it, they would embrace the idea. They'd get excited and I'd see them put up another item up for rent.'

Steve also created demand in the other direction. After collecting catalogues from major department stores, he identified the items he believed would be in demand as rentals. He listed all these products on the site and when people rented the item via the website, he went out and bought that item at the department store. 'Then I rented it and gave the renter an exceptional user experience. After the transaction I sold the item on eBay for about 80 per cent of the retail price and recouped my costs.

'I had to do a few risky things to prove that there is a place for this service in society. And if you have a start-up, you've got to be prepared to contribute to some of the pieces that build the story. Don't just wait for the story to unfold. You're the narrator. It's your start-up, and you have the power to create whatever story you want to tell about it.'

Your actions

Your pitch story

When your business is centred on a new concept it can be exhilarating. The possibilities are endless; the opportunity to scale is unlimited; and you truly think this could be the Next Big Thing. And it probably will be, but it will get there only if everyone else understands what you are so excited about. So take a chill pill, take an outsider's view of your start-up and imagine that you need to explain your business to a sceptic. Follow these steps or download your Pitch Story template in the exclusive resources section at <www.powerstoriesbook.com>.

1 Can you clearly express how your idea or business solves a big problem?
2 Can you demonstrate that you're in for the long haul?
3 Use the answers to points 1 and 2 to create your overall pitch.
4 Now tailor your pitch to different groups, such as your customers, family and employees.
5 Start having those 100 coffees!

CHAPTER 7

Your product story

I confess. I have a fetish. It's clean. It's bare. It's oh-so-seductive. And I'd pretty much pay anything for it.

I'm talking about … stationery. That's right, paper, but not just any paper. Beautiful notebooks with blank pages ready to be touched. Smooth, pristine canvases just waiting to be stained by that first drop of ink.

I've had this affliction for years. Come to my home and you'll find drawers full of blank notebooks, in all shapes and sizes. Leather bound, wrapped in cloth, silk embroidered, embossed with gold stamping and, more recently, laser engraved.

I know I'm not the only person in the world with a penchant for blank notebooks. And if you are the same, you probably understand the romance of buying a Moleskine. While the potential in those blank pages plays a part in the seduction, so does the story behind the Moleskine experience. You're reminded of this story every time you tear off the plastic wrapping that's kept your Moleskine notebook pristine and a little booklet drops out of the pages. It's here—in

English with translations in French, Spanish and Italian—that the Moleskine story is told.

You've probably heard it before: 'The legendary notebook…used by artists and thinkers over the past two centuries: among them Vincent van Gogh, Pablo Picasso, Ernest Hemingway and Bruce Chatwin.'

There's a romance to the idea that you are using the same creative tools as these greats. That what you record on those precious pages—words, sketches, ideas—may some day reach the same heights. You'll see the reference to these artists on blogs, fan sites and comments from Moleskine devotees all over the world. It's a marketing strategy that clearly works. Moleskines are sold through about 22 000 retailers, and its turnover grew from €80 million in 2006 to more than €200 million in 2010.

Every time that little booklet falls out of a new Moleskine, we fan our thumb over the pages of the notebook, smell the freshness of the new sheets of paper and cast our eyes over the story again. And those words jump out: 'legendary notebook…Vincent van Gogh…' But set the romance aside and read it again, carefully. Go on. Read the full sentence. It actually says:

> The Moleskine notebook is the heir and successor to the legendary notebook used by artists and thinkers over the past two centuries: among them Vincent van Gogh, Pablo Picasso, Ernest Hemingway and Bruce Chatwin.

'Heir and successor.' Not the real thing. That wouldn't be possible because the Moleskine only began production in 1997, by a small Milanese company called Modo & Modo. By then van Gogh, Picasso, Hemingway and even Chatwin were long gone—and unable to attest to whether they were true fans of the notebook.

Many artists in the late 19th and early 20th centuries used little black notebooks that were common in Europe at the time. But Moleskine's association with these artists is almost like saying that the popular IKEA flatpacked BILLY bookcase (found in shared houses and student dorms all over the world) is the 'heir and successor' to one used by Mozart. Because chances are he had a bookcase that looked a bit the same. And before it was assembled, you could probably lay all the pieces out on the ground flat.

Modo & Modo founder Francesco Franceschi told the *International Herald Tribune* in 2004: 'It's an exaggeration. It's marketing, not science. It's not the absolute truth.'

The myth of 'Hemingway's notebook' has been perpetuated by countless Moleskine-lovers all over the world. There's the truth. And then there's the story you want to believe.

Whether or not you bought into the Moleskine story, or agree with its 'exaggeration', one thing's for sure. It's an idea that sticks. I mean, let's be serious. It's a glorified exercise book. Sure, it's a nice size. You can slip it into your briefcase or handbag and the pages rarely fall out. But let's get real, Hemingway did not use it. It is, though, a great example of how a story can make or break a product. Do you think the Moleskine would be as successful if it was marketed as 'a small, black rectangular notebook with rounded edges and pages, some of which are glued and others stitched'? Hell, no.

When it comes to selling your products, it pays to ensure that you've crafted the next power story you need: your Product Story.

What should be in your product story?

So what's involved in your product story? What if you don't want to associate your widget with a bunch of famous dead people, even if it will gain your product a cult following? Well, your product story actually has two fairly distinct parts. Think of them as:

- *Your internal story:* creating your product.
- *Your external story:* selling your product.

Of course, your internal story applies only if you created the product, whether it is a tangible object (like an iPhone cover), something more ephemeral (like software) or a service (like when your accountant does your tax return). If you play an intermediary role, such as a retailer who buys from a manufacturer and sells to the consumer, your internal story may not be so relevant.

Your internal story: creating your product

According to Twitter co-founder Jack Dorsey, you should use storytelling as an integral part of the creation process. After Jack co-founded the ubiquitous social networking service in 2006, he went on to found electronic payments company Square in 2009. Speaking at the Entrepreneurial Thought Leaders lecture series from Stanford Technology Ventures, Jack said: 'One of the biggest things that has helped me is learning how to become a better storyteller—and the power of a story.'

It's vital to put yourself in the shoes of the person using the product, he explained. Many businesses can get caught up in developing features and adding bells and whistles that may not be needed, or appreciated, by the ultimate users.

'We spend a lot of time writing what's called user narratives,' said Jack. This means describing the user experience. Imagine who your user is. Give them a name. Picture what they look like. Let's say you come up with a user you'll call Graham. Anticipate the situations in which Graham will use the product and identify how he would expect the product to help him. It doesn't matter whether you are creating a tech-related product (as Jack did with Square) or a more traditional widget, when you get it right, said Jack, 'it reads like play. It's really, really beautiful.'

Jack discovered that by getting the story right you're able to streamline the product creation process. It's a way of getting all disparate inputs—from engineers and operations to marketing—to play their part in the same story. 'If you do that story well, then all of the prioritisation—all of the product, all of the design and all of the coordination that you need to do with these products—just falls out naturally…everyone can relate to the story from all levels of the organisation.'

You don't have to be a billion-dollar company like Twitter or Square to use storytelling in your product creation. If you are a small business creating a new product that requires input from suppliers, contractors and staff, they all need to understand the big picture. They need to see what role they are playing in the overall story in order to be able to do it well.

When you're an entrepreneur, *you* might have a clear idea of how everyone fits in. You might already have painted the big picture in your mind and know exactly what needs to be done, and by whom. Even if you're a control freak who likes being the puppeteer, pulling the strings of everyone in your cast of characters, this is simply exhausting. It's also high risk—if you're sick or incapacitated, the show does *not* go on.

Still, it can be useful to approach the product creation process as a play, with you as director. You brief everyone on the overall vision of what you want to achieve, assign everyone their parts, empower them with a script that will serve as an overall guide for the story. As director, you'll still shape and guide how it progresses, but come opening night the story can still be told—even if you can't be there.

'We want to tell an epic story,' Jack said. 'We want to solve a really big problem. We don't want to have a bunch of short stories strung together. We want one epic cohesive story that we tell the world. And both Twitter and Square are driving towards this goal.'

The story surrounding the creation of your product is less about creativity than about clarity. It's simply about having a clear understanding of what the product is and what it's supposed to achieve.

Your external story: selling your product (the four Bs)

Once you have a product ready for sale, this is where the creativity kicks in, and this is where you get to experiment with the four Bs. Because, depending on how complex or everyday your product is, you may need to consider using some or all of these stories.

Brief explanation

It sounds simple, but the number of business owners who can't distil their product into a sentence astounds me. Hell, I'll even live with two sentences.

Recently, a small business owner (we'll call her Lydia) came to me for advice about her business. Lydia said she had a great idea but it just wasn't getting traction. 'I don't have problems getting meetings with people. I go to countless meetings every week, but no-one is signing up. I don't know what I'm doing wrong,' she said.

I asked her to tell me about her product. She started talking—and 20 minutes later I politely interrupted and asked her to stop.

'Is this the explanation you give when you go to meetings?' I asked.

She nodded.

I looked at her, not entirely sure how to phrase what I wanted to say next. Internally, it went something like: 'Are you kidding me? You've been talking non-stop for 20 minutes and I know you're nowhere near the end of your explanation and I still have absolutely no clue what you're selling.'

She read my mind. 'I know, I know. People need to understand how it works, but that explanation takes a while to get through.'

This was Lydia's first mistake. When someone is presented with your product for the first time, they don't need to understand how it works. They just need know *what it is* and *what it can do for them*. When I buy a car, I could care less about how the electronic stability control interacts with the brake assist. I simply *assume* that it does.

'So can you help me make my explanation shorter?' said Lydia.

I workshopped her business right there on the spot, even if just to save her next unsuspecting prospect from losing half an hour of their life they'll never get back.

It took several questions, and each time she felt compelled to explain the inner workings of her product. Various phrases permeated the fog of words: 'monthly subscription ... or it's lower if you take the annual option ... great for sporting clubs ... community groups ... such great discounts ... cater specifically for families ... the more people, the better the deals ... pass on the savings to members ... different membership levels ... no obligation to buy ... just a great opportunity ...'

Dear God, please make this long-winded explanation stop.

When Lydia finally drew a breath, I tried to make sense of the word salad she'd tossed at me. Still unsure if I had understood it correctly, I ventured a guess.

'So, it sounds like a ... loyalty program? I asked.

She stopped, almost taken aback. 'Well, yes. I guess it is.'

'And when people join, they get ... discounts?'

She nodded, smiling, as though pleased she had got her point across.

'And those discounts are on things ... that are good for ... families?'

'That's it exactly!' she said excitedly.

I smiled and let her words hang in the air. She cottoned on.

'Well, that's really what I should say to people, shouldn't I?'

Lydia appeared to be energised by this revelation and began gathering her brochures, fact sheets and application forms. 'I've got to get started,' she said. 'Thank you so much for your time, it's been so helpful. I've got more appointments to make!' And with that she was gone.

Now you don't need a session with me to figure out a brief explanation of your product. I barely said a word anyway. Lydia worked it out for herself. It's simple, because it all boils down to this:

- What is your product?
- How does it help people?

If you find that your explanation resembles an interminable commentary from Eddie McGuire more than a brief description of your product, then you need to keep distilling it until you can answer each of those two questions in a single sentence.

Birth of an idea

A \$100 trillion note. I'm holding a \$100 trillion note! That's \$100 000 000 000 000. Seriously. Look at all those zeros. I hand it back to Tony Wheeler, who slides it back into his wallet, shaking his head at the fact inflation in Zimbabwe can result in paper money featuring numbers that barely fit on the paper they're printed on. Tony said: 'About two years ago, the one hundred trillion dollar note was worth about \$30. Six months later, it was worth 30 cents.'

The banknote was the latest memento from his travels, a passion that spawned the Lonely Planet empire of guidebooks, magazines, a television production company and mobile apps. The business had its beginnings in conversations that Tony and his wife Maureen had with people in Australia after they had travelled overland from London to Sydney in 1972. After being quizzed for tips on where to stay and what to see, the couple decided to take the meticulous notes Tony had kept throughout the trip and turn them into a book.

Their first book, *Across Asia on the Cheap*, came out in October 1973 priced at A\$1.80. It was typed and cobbled together in their home and hand delivered to bookstores. Five hundred destination guidebooks later, Lonely Planet has become a dominant force in the travel guidebook industry. The Wheelers sold the business to the BBC (75 per cent in 2007 and the rest in 2011).

The story of the birth of the business has become legendary, even inspiring a 2011 travel memoir, *Tell Them to Get Lost — Travels With the Lonely Planet Guidebook That Started it All*, by Brian Thacker about his visit to Asia with nothing to guide him but an original copy of the first book. It's a story that gives the Lonely Planet brand credibility and underpins what the company stands for. Fans of Lonely Planet guidebooks aren't just buying a book full of listings. They're buying into a lifestyle—one that represents freedom and adventure, and travel.

Even if your story isn't as exotic as Tony's, it can be powerful to articulate the story behind the birth of your idea or product.

'Where did you get the idea for that?' It's a question we ask entrepreneurs all the time. And we ask it because we're fascinated to hear the story of how a mere thought can eventually turn into a tangible product. We want to find out about how a product's journey began. When you share details about the 'birth' of the product, it can add credibility, entertainment value or just the right amount of quirkiness to make your product memorable. Even if you weren't involved in the product's creation, try to find out the story behind the idea. It may be the very story that connects with people.

Benefits versus features

Last time I moved house, I wanted to get rid of a lot of my furniture because I didn't think it suited the look and feel of my new place. So I wanted to ensure that I offloaded my unwanted pieces well before moving day. That's when I became friends with eBay.

At the time, I was an eBay virgin. But after my first time, I loved it. And I was ready to come back for more. One of my first listings was a three-piece outdoor setting that sat on the balcony of my apartment. When I sold it a week later, for the same price I'd bought it for a year before, I was hooked. Within two weeks I had sold a sofa, clothes rack, dining table, coffee table and boxing bag—all of them nearly reaching the price I had originally paid. I had to stop myself from listing practically everything that wasn't nailed down in my apartment. What auction fairyland had I stumbled into? Why had I not already embraced this eBay of which so many people spoke so highly?

My friend Vanessa, a prolific eBayer, assured me this was not normal. 'I can't believe the prices you're getting for your crap.'

'It's not crap!' I said defensively.

Vanessa checked out my remaining items for sale. 'Wow, it's your descriptions! Who writes this kind of thing?'

I've since realised that a three-piece outdoor setting is likely to be listed like this:

3-piece outdoor setting
Aluminium frame round table with white glass table top. 72 cm height x 90 cm wide. Two aluminium frame chairs with netted seat. One year old. Excellent condition.

But as a writer I couldn't help but tell a story, so I wrote something like this.

Imagine coming home after a long day. Imagine relaxing on your new outdoor setting with a glass of wine in your hand as you watch the sun set, taking the stresses of your day with it. Imagine dining al fresco by candlelight with friends on balmy summer evenings. Or chilling out with the weekend newspapers and a freshly brewed cup of coffee while basking in the winter sun.

With a glass table top in mint condition, this setting is only 12 months old. Easy to clean, its green aluminium frame blends into any outdoor environment. I use my outdoor setting on my compact Balinese-inspired balcony. But this classic design will be ideal whether you have a small space or want to create an intimate nook within a much bigger area …

You get the idea. Hey, I didn't know any better. I realise now that this is not the way most people list their junky items on eBay, but it seemed to be getting me results—which also illustrated the power of story. I wasn't just listing a series of features, I was helping prospective buyers visualise what they could do with the outdoor setting. I focused on the benefits of the setting, not the features. And the bids just kept getting higher and higher. I know I'm not winning any literature prizes for it, but it gets me great prices for my unwanted items!

When you are telling a story about your product, consider whether the features or the benefits are going to resonate more with a prospective buyer. In most cases, it's more powerful to explain the benefits.

Here are a couple of examples:

A microphone ...

Features: DVCam directional condensor microphone
Benefits: This microphone is great if you're interviewing someone and you don't want to pick up background noise.

A skin care product ...

Features: This formula contains benzoyl peroxide to penetrate pores.
Benefits: This formula contains ingredients to help you get the great skin you want, now.

When you're describing your product or service, explain its benefits—the impact it's going to have on your customers' lives. I'm not suggesting you shouldn't include technical specifications, as they can be important. Just make sure you *also* tell a story.

Brand

Tell the stories that reinforce your brand. Of course, that means you first need to be clear on what your brand stands for. In the simplest terms, your brand is what people say about you when you're not around.

'Oh, they're very cool. On the pulse. Very street smart. Great design.'
'Incredible after-sales service. They will go out of their way to help you. They're just so nice.'
'Very polite. Very conservative. Every customer gets a thankyou note on monogrammed paper.'
'They're expensive. But they're the best.'
'So cheap—it's great! Buy 10 of everything. And you can negotiate. But don't expect to get served in a hurry.'

What does your brand stand for? Imagine the conversations people are having about you when you're not around. The scary part here is if you imagine these conversations but then don't like what you're hearing. If that's the case, then you know there's something wrong and you need to start repairing your brand.

So decide on the conversations you *want* to hear. Imagine your business is exactly where you want it to be: operations area streamlined, customer service the best it's ever been, and you have a product range to die for. Even if you haven't reached this point yet in reality, imagine the conversations people are having about you now. Then make sure that the product stories you tell reinforce the brand that you want to be.

So what does that actually look like? Well, if your brand is about 'good value' and 'cost efficiency', your stories might include how you've secured a bulk shipment of widgets so you can pass on the cost savings to customers. If your brand is about luxury and decadence, then you might want to tweet or blog pictures of your product at fancy events or being used by high-society types.

Online product descriptions

One of the most important places where your product story needs to be front and centre is your website, particularly if you have an online store. With people increasingly using Google as their first port of call to find out about products, you need to ensure that your product story is there to convince and convert them when they are searching for the information. Don't assume that people will call if they want to find out more or head into your physical store if they want to see and touch your product. If your site doesn't provide the information consumers need *but your competitor's site does*, no guesses as to where most consumers will end up buying.

Trade shows and in-store displays

Certain products are best showcased at a trade show or exhibition or in store. That might be because the best way to reach people is to allow them to see, touch and feel your product. But it's important not to forget to make the most of your product story.

I've been to countless trade shows and am often amazed that so many businesses simply waste their time and money being there. In some cases, it's apparent to me they're never going to make it big.

They might have the best product in the world, but that counts for little if they can't communicate what that product is actually about. So what mistakes can you avoid if you find yourself in a similar situation?

Use helpful signage
These days, whacking up a big sign of your groovy logo isn't going to cut it. This might work if you have a self-explanatory name like Byron Bay Cookie Company. But if you're a start-up that has adopted a Google-type name such as Moovr, Kleenr or Mophie, it's vital that you have a tagline that explains to consumers what this linguistic invention actually represents.

Choose knowledgeable representatives
If you want people to find out more about your product, make sure your representatives are well versed in what it can do. They need to learn your product story. Don't let an exchange like this happen:

> Me: 'Can you tell me about your product?'
> Them: 'Ummm … We're still in beta.'
> Me: 'Okay, what does it do?'
> Them: 'It's like an app.'
> Me: 'What does the app do?'
> Them: 'We have almost 10 000 subscribers.'
> Me (trying a different tack): 'Maybe you can *show* me what your
> app does.'
> Them: 'Sure … Oh, actually this screen just shows some screenshots
> we slapped together yesterday. We don't have a live demo.'

I'll spare you the whole conversation, but you get the idea. It happened at a trade show I attended. It confounds me that a business would fork over much-needed cash to secure a booth with exposure to thousands of people in their target market and then basically squander the opportunity.

Craft a script and FAQs
If you are roping in helpers who may not be clued up about your product or service, then create a script and a list of frequently asked

questions and answers so it doesn't look like your team is a pack of dummies. Role-play some likely scenarios and potential enquiries so your representatives get some practice in answering questions about the product.

Ensure you have printed marketing materials on hand

Ensure you have some printed marketing materials available for customers who might be genuinely interested in what you have to offer. You might think it's cool just to go with a striking graphic and groovy logo, simply because it looks good. But you would be doing yourself a disservice. I've heard entrepreneurs say: 'But if people are interested, they can find out everything at our website. What's the point of replicating it here?'

Oh dear. I want to take these people by the shoulders and shake them. If you're a fledgling company that no-one knows about, you need to *do everything you can* to get people interested in what you do. Unless you're as famous as Coke, you need to craft an enticing message, identify the problem your product or service is likely to solve and give people a reason to visit your site to find out more.

Trade shows can be extremely valuable opportunities to meet new customers and prospects. You get to chat one-on-one. You can demo your product and get instant feedback without having to make a single cold call. But you can't just front up and hope for the best. This is one situation where you can't rely on: 'Build it and they will come.'

If you want to make the most of this opportunity, ensure you've crafted your product story and ensure that you tell it. This power story will help you present your product in the best light and may even gain you a new legion of fans.

I see too many business owners neglect storytelling when it comes to products. But this is a power story that shouldn't be overlooked. We don't pay enough attention to our products—and their stories—because it's easy to relegate them to mere inventory items that have to be offloaded. In some cases, though, your products have a unique story all their own that can have a profound impact on people. If you are serious about increasing sales and growing your business, it's vital to identify and share those stories.

Your actions

Your product story

Place your product in front of you. If you are selling a service or an intangible item such as software, use an item that represents it. You're about to create your product story. Follow these steps or download your Product Story template in the exclusive resources section at <www.powerstoriesbook.com>.

1 Who will use your product? If you're creating a product or service, create your user narrative. Who are they? How old are they? How will they use the product? What will they like and dislike about it?

2 Have you written brief explanations of all your products? Think of them as each item's very own elevator pitch.

3 Does your product have a quirky or fascinating story behind its creation? Where are the ideal places to tell this story (swing tag on clothes, website, brochure in store, YouTube video)?

4 Write down a list of the product's features, then write about the benefits people get from these features.

5 Identify the stories about your product that will reinforce your brand.

CHAPTER 8

Your leader's story

Emma Stevenson packed up her life in Australia and headed for New York in March 2012. She made the decision to move to the other side of the world only four weeks before getting on the plane. Leaving her friends, family and career in Newcastle, two hours north of Sydney, for a new life, Emma didn't care if she went to New York or New Delhi. She would have gone anywhere to work with *charity: water*. For no money.

It's a big move for the 24-year-old, who was working as a school teacher before she stumbled on the story of *charity: water*'s Scott Harrison while browsing the internet.

'I read their blog for hours and scanned through all the photos of the people whose lives were changing as a result of their work,' says Emma. 'I watched their videos and stories from the field. When you see children get clean water for the first time … you can't put a price on that.'

It was a story that inspired her to move continents and dedicate her time to work for the cause for free. Thanks to a kind relative who gave her $9000, she can afford to do this for a while until she figures out how to earn an income.

It happens to be World Water Day (22 March) when I step into *charity: water*'s offices in Lower Manhattan, New York. The offices look more like a groovy art gallery than a not-for-profit. But the artworks on the expansive white walls aren't funky canvases with postmodern themes created by emerging New York artists. They are huge photos of people in remote villages in developing countries, many accessing clean water for the first time. They feature young faces drinking from newly installed pumps and drilling rigs hitting underground sources of clean water. A large screen features a Twitter feed whenever a tweet about *charity: water* is posted. Rows of yellow jerry cans, the organisation's symbol of hope, line the wall.

Here Emma stays in the office late, contributing ideas, working hard—and loving every minute of it. 'This is more than just an internship,' she says. 'This is a very core part of my life.'

It's the kind of loyalty and motivation that any leader would love to see in their team members, particularly those that *do* get paid. Such commitment can result from an authentic and inspiring Leader's Story. It's this power story that you need to master if you want other people to buy into your vision and help make it a reality. But whether you are the leader of a charity, a small business or a large organisation, the five elements of your leader's story are the same:

- Show people who you are.
- Determine what's different about your organisation or business.
- Inspire people to action.
- Educate and inform.
- Share simple messages.

Show people who you are

Before they can be persuaded to get behind your vision, people need to know, like and trust you. So if they're not already familiar with you, let them get to know you. This means revealing aspects of your life or experiences that demonstrate what you stand for, what's important to you, what your values are.

Typically, a leader has a vision. That might be to bring clean drinking water to communities who lack it, to galvanise a community to save a local national park, or to motivate a team during a difficult period of the business. As a leader, you may think that your vision is obvious, and you can't imagine anyone who wouldn't buy into it. After all, don't we all want clean drinking water or safe parks? If a company is struggling because of the economic climate, doesn't everyone want to pull together so we can all keep our jobs?

The short answer to that is: no. People have different priorities. Everyone has a different agenda, and everyone has a different opinion on what constitutes a worthwhile vision. You might have the noblest vision in the world, but it's a moot point if you can't get the support you need.

That was the challenge that faced Scott Harrison when he decided he wanted to tackle the world water crisis. Born in Philadelphia and raised in New Jersey, Scott spent much of his twenties as a nightclub promoter, living a decadent lifestyle surrounded by drink, drugs and fast living. At 28, he went through a crisis of conscience. He felt emotionally, spiritually and morally bankrupt, and decided his life needed to change.

Scott went to Africa as a photojournalist with the charity Mercy Ships, which operates hospital ships, staffed by volunteer doctors, dentists and other medical professionals, that provide free medical surgeries to the world's poorest nations. It was during his time in Liberia that he became aware of the water crisis. There he saw polluted, scum-filled ponds infested with bugs and learned that such ponds were the primary water sources for many people. Investigating further, Scott discovered that up to 80 per cent of diseases were caused by lack of water and poor sanitation.

After spending a couple of years volunteering with Mercy Ships, Scott returned to New York with his heart on fire to change the world. 'Everything changed for me when I walked down that gangway. I never had another cigarette—and I had smoked two packs [a day] for 10 or 11 years. I quit gambling, quit porn, never set foot in a strip club, quit all drugs,' Scott said in an interview with tech media personality Kevin Rose.

'I wanted to do two things before I died. I wanted to make sure that everybody on Earth had access to clean water … and I really wanted to give people a charity they could believe in. I wanted to reinvent the space for people my age who were jaded and cynical.'

For Scott Harrison, an essential part of his story is the life he used to live as a hedonistic party animal who drank, got high, gambled, and earned and spent a fortune. It's an important part of the story because his turnaround was so dramatic. It shows where he came from and what he learned from the experience. People are fascinated: they empathise, they understand and they want to cheer him on.

If you're a leader, the days of hiding in an ivory tower are long gone. You need to let people get to know you, connect with your vision and understand what you stand for. Your stories can't just be about your plans and ambitions—make sure they're about you as well. But don't fall into the trap of thinking that a chronological autobiography will do the trick. Instead, focus on the stories that reveal what you believe in and why you do what you do. These are often stories about turning points in your life, how you've overcome challenges and why you've chosen the path you're on.

Determine what's different about your organisation or business

If you want people to support your organisation, the vehicle through which you're achieving your vision, then they need to trust the organisation in addition to trusting you. They also need to know what it means to deal with your company. How will they be treated? How are your employees treated? What kind of track record do you have?

Scott started *charity: water* in 2006, on his thirty-first birthday. He threw a party, invited 700 friends and charged them each $20. They raised almost $15000, enough to drill three wells in Uganda, and when they were built, Scott sent pictures of the wells to all the party attendees so they could see what their money had bought.

This was the start of *charity: water*, a non-profit organisation that brings clean water to developing countries. It began modestly, run out of his lounge room, but Scott was clear from the start that to change the world he had to build a powerful brand. 'I thought if we're going to solve a problem as big as the global water crisis, we need an epic brand,' he said. That's because Scott has epic ambitions. By the end of 2011, *charity: water* had provided clean drinking water to 2 million people. Its goal for 2020 is to reach 100 million people. According to *charity: water*, one in nine people in the world doesn't have access to clean water. That's nearly a billion people whose only access to water may be a polluted river, ditch or swamp, sometimes a three-hour walk away.

From its humble beginnings, *charity: water* now has 26 employees and a team of volunteers. For the organisation to work, Scott has to inspire his team to get behind his vision, and together, they spread the *charity: water* story to inspire other people to do the same.

There is no argument that for most charities the goal is noble. However, the not-for-profit sector often comes under fire for the high proportion of funds raised that may be diverted to administrative expenses. Scott nips this problem in the bud with a policy that 100 per cent of public donations go directly to the water projects in the field. All the organisation's operating expenses, such as salaries or rent, are funded through private donors and sponsors.

It would be easy for cynics who visit the *charity: water* office to think otherwise. After all, it's in a hip area of New York and it looks pretty cool. But they help set that story straight as soon as you step through the door, where a plaque states:

1 Newmark Knight Frank gave us an incredible space we could never afford.
2 Steelcase filled our office with desks, chairs and whiteboards.
3 InterfaceFLOR cut down the noise by donating carpet tiles.
4 Cisco donated phones and network servers, keeping us connected.
5 RCN gave us free internet so we could share our stories with the world.
6 Castor hooked us up with fabulous lighting.
7 Thomas Beale built our very first conference room table.
8 Robert Valentine helped design our space and gave us his very best furniture.
9 GSG and Peeq Media printed large-scale photographs for our walls.
10 We bought ping pong table because we need a break from time to time.

The organisation makes a point of emphasising its financial probity and integrity. It tells clear and pointed stories about 'the way they do things' to minimise misinterpretation about fund-raising and money management.

As a leader, you already have an intimate knowledge of your organisation, but most people won't have this luxury. Think about the stories you need to tell to showcase what your company is about. If you want someone to become a key supplier to your company, you might focus on stories that reflect your plans for the future and how their role will expand when these plans come to fruition. If you want to attract an employee, you'll tell stories about other employees and their journey with your organisation. And if you are looking to sign up a client, your stories might reflect the impact you've had on other clients' lives.

Inspire people to action

Once you've fostered a connection, you probably want people to take action. You need to give people the tools to do this.

At *charity: water* this is done by empowering regular supporters to be heroes in their own story. They can do this by 'pledging' their birthday. *charity: water* provides an online platform where you can set up a donation page and ask your friends to donate cash instead of plying you with gifts on your big day. The average 'birthday pledge' results in a $1000 donation, made up of all the smaller donations from your friends. But instead of this donation disappearing into a general pool of funds, *charity: water* makes sure that's not the end of your story. You stay engaged, because when the project is complete you're sent a URL to a web page. Here you can see, via photos or videos and GPS marker, exactly what you've built and where it is. You can share that URL with the friends who donated money for your birthday, so they can be part of the story too. *charity: water* makes it easy for you to become a hero in your own story. You've made a difference, and hopefully, as a result, you'll do it again next year.

As a leader, your story is not about you being the hero. It's about letting other people become heroes in their own stories. Empower others to take action but, as important, champion them when they do. Publicly pat them on the back, highlight their contributions and share *their* stories with your community.

Like the seven-year-old boy in Austin, Texas, who pledged his birthday and door-knocked in his neighbourhood asking for $7 to raise funds for *charity: water*—he collected $22 000. Or the guys who climbed Mount Kilimanjaro and raised $30 000. Or the scrapbookers who raised $50 000. People have raised money doing everything from skydiving and kite surfing to walking across America. Scott said: 'Crazy stories started popping up all around the world as all these people said, "I don't have a lot of money to give, but maybe I can go and do something totally creative and get my community involved".'

Rachel Beckwith, a young girl in Bellevue, Washington, had heard the story of *charity: water*. Rachel said there were only two people in the world she really wanted to meet: Lady Gaga and Scott Harrison. She decided to pledge her ninth birthday, on 12 June 2011, to the cause, set up a donation page and asked her friends and family to donate instead of giving her presents. Rachel hoped to raise $300. She came close to her goal, reaching $220. Five weeks later, she was in a multi-car highway pile-up and was taken to hospital. On 23 July 2011, her life support was turned off. When the news spread, donations poured into her *charity: water* page from all over the world. By 12 August the campaign crossed the $1 million mark. When the campaign was closed on 1 October, $1 271 713 had been raised—enough to bring clean water to 84 780 people in developing countries.

Educate and inform

Once you've given people the tools to take action, you need to communicate how to *use* those tools. Otherwise, it's like setting a car engine and a toolbox in front of a novice without giving them any instruction on what to do next.

As a leader, you have to educate and inform in order to motivate people. The concept of pledging a birthday is fairly easy to grasp, but leaders are often faced with far more complex issues. Maybe you need to show your team how to use a complex new computer system. Or you need to get your staff to provide specific details about their superannuation funds and asset allocation choices. Or maybe you have to show your sales team how to measure the impact of import duty on their profit margins.

If you want people to follow particular procedures or processes, you obviously need to provide clear step-by-step instructions. But there's a far better chance that these instructions will actually be followed if you package them with a story.

Let's take the computer system example. It can be tempting to document the various steps users need to take in order to use the new features, complete with screenshots, all packaged in a PDF, but what are the chances of people actually reading it? It's more meaningful to outline a scenario in which they will use the new computer system. Who would be involved? Why would the system be useful? What's a likely consequence if it's not executed? How much time will it save? Creating a story around it not only makes it easier for people to understand why it's needed; it also provides a framework within which they can remember the instructions.

Share simple messages

Your leader's story doesn't have to be complex. You don't need reams of data and piles of reports to convince someone to take action. If you want to reach as many people as possible, keep it simple and authentic.

On World Water Day, Paull Young has his work cut out for him. When I first met Paull in Sydney several years ago he was a young public relations professional who was making a name for himself consulting to large companies on how to use social media. With clients like Telstra, Citrix and *The New York Times*, Paull scored a job at a New York-based social business consultancy. But in September 2008 he heard the *charity: water* story and pledged his birthday.

By May 2010 he knew he wanted to work for the organisation, so he joined as director of digital engagement. But sharing the *charity: water* story isn't just about sending a few tweets about giving up your birthday. It's a strategic, calculated marketing plan that has produced great results. Because in case you haven't noticed, they have big goals at *charity: water*. They want to end the world water crisis. This means they plan to raise $25 million in 2012. And $100 million in 2015.

So on World Water Day, Paull goes all out to secure as many birthday pledges as he can for the year. His goal is 12 000 pledges in 2012. And if all those who pledge come through with the goods, he has raised $12 million.

The digital campaign actually starts well before World Water Day, reaching out to key influencers, such as celebrities and high-profile Silicon Valley entrepreneurs, people who have previously donated more than $5000 or simply those with a huge social media following. 'We reached out ahead of time by sending out emails about what our goal is and to encourage them to share the message about World Water Day in their own networks,' says Paull.

It's a message that's obviously working, as by the next morning celebrities from Justin Bieber and Mike Tyson to Alyssa Milano and Melanie Griffith have tweeted messages supporting *charity: water*. They tweet, their friends retweet and the hashtag #worldwaterday is trending. The message starts to spread.

About 20 staff and volunteers — most of them in their twenties — converge on *charity: water*'s boardroom, where Paull heads up a coordinated effort to spread the word far and wide. A series of clocks line the wall. But the cities featured underneath each clock are not those you'll find in most corporate boardrooms: New York, London, Hong Kong, Paris. Instead, these clocks represent times in Tegucigalpa, Honduras; Port-au-Prince, Haiti; Monrovia, Liberia; Bangui, Central African Republic; Addis Ababa, Ethiopia; New Delhi, India; and Dhaka, Bangladesh. These are the places where *charity: water* is making a difference.

Volunteers flick between screens, checking out mentions of *charity: water* on Twitter streams, Facebook, Instagram — and every other social media platform in between. They all access a centralised Google Docs file, and are busy sharing pre-written tweets and Facebook status updates about *charity: water* to their own networks, hoping their friends will also spread the word. The centralised file also contains sample email templates that volunteers are encouraged to personalise and send to their contacts.

By 11 am 1000 people have pledged their birthdays. With the average donation being $1000, that's $1 million raised in just over two hours. And the day is young. Music is blaring from the speakers and the people in the room tap away at the keyboards with a quiet energy that builds as the day goes on.

'It's 11 am in New York, so California's not awake yet. We should see a spike in a couple of hours.'

'Someone just wrote on Facebook: "Today is a great day because it's World Water Day. I won't give up my next birthday but I'll donate $1000 to charity: water".'

'Are we getting traffic from Pinterest?'

'We're trending in New York City.'

'Check out this tweet: "Scott Harrison looks like the dude from Inception".'

'Do we know the open rates from last night's email?'

Rihanna's latest song comes over the speakers and one of the volunteers starts humming.

'Did you know that Rihanna has over 14 million followers?'

'Shall we tweet her about this?'

This is not your average charity, or at least not the stereotype of what a traditional charity looks like. *charity: water* is writing its own story about how a charity can work.

Although it's easy to use technology to send automatic 'thanks' to donors or to email everyone on a database en masse, Paull says *charity: water*'s approach is more personalised. 'It's about developing a relationship. When you donate, you're not just a number. If you donate, someone here will write back to you. If you tweet that you've pledged your birthday, we'll "favourite" your tweet to support you in return.' The strategy is to 'inspire through content', Paull explains. 'If you create great content then people will share it for you. Think of it as a series of concentric circles: we share it with our core audience, they share it with their friends—and so on.

'We have a culture led by storytelling. Our founder, Scott, is pure storyteller. The key is to have amazing content all the time. My job is to share it with the world.'

On *charity: water*'s fifth birthday, Scott Harrison recorded a video to show followers what had been achieved. You can find it in the exclusive resources section at <www.powerstoriesbook.com>. As a leader, he spoke directly to his community of followers. Part of his message on camera was:

> You did incredible things to raise money. You biked. You ran. You walked across America. You skated and surfed. You sang and you danced. You sold lemonade and recycled. You gave up thousands of birthdays and asked for donations instead of gifts.
>
> We sent your money around the world, and people started working. Drilling rigs rolled into villages, and drillers found clean water underground. Women walked less and got hours of wasted time back each day. They spent more time with their children, and some started small businesses.
>
> Kids stopped drinking water that made them sick. And spent more time in school. Everyone was healthier. Happier.
>
> Water changed everything.

In only five years, you took a simple story and did more than we ever thought possible. You helped us bring clean water to two million people in 19 countries.

So what's next? …

Ensure you have another story

Scott asks his community: *So what's next?* When your story is done, what better way to keep people engaged than with a sequel? In the video, Scott continues by explaining the next step in the *charity: water* journey, showing them how to continue their story.

Emma Stevenson is keen to be part of that story. 'I don't know that I can accurately explain my experience here, but it has been undeniably the most amazing thing I have ever done with my life,' she says of her internship. 'I feel like people believe in me here. It is an organisation that believes in the power of one, they inspire you to think creatively and battle against the odds. But most of all they tell stories of hope. In a world that is so desperately seeking help it is so easy to get overwhelmed by the problems rather then inspired by the stories of triumph. I want to be part of the solution.'

Most stories *about* leaders highlight how they galvanise armies into action, create a unique vision to build a company or, through personal strength and determination, achieve an insurmountable goal against all odds. As a leader, the power story you can *tell* is the one where you cast your followers in the role of hero. Once they get behind your vision, let them create their own story. Empower them. Believe in them. Give them the opportunity to make a difference — in growing your business, in transforming their own lives, and even in changing the world.

Your actions

Your leader's story

As an entrepreneur, you are a leader. Make no bones about it, when you are running a business, you need to step up and accept that you are the one steering the ship. But, as we've seen, that doesn't necessarily mean you are the one who needs to be in the limelight. As a leader, you need to set aside time to craft your stories, because it's these stories that will move and inspire people into action.

Follow these steps or download your Leader's Story template in the exclusive resources section at <www.powerstoriesbook. com>.

1 How can you show people who you are? Consider three new ways in which you can give people an insight into your personality or values.
2 Write down how your organisation is different from others. Determine where you can use this statement (website, business card, social media and so on).
3 Determine what actions you most want your followers to take and then do an audit of whether you have actually equipped them with the right tools. When you've identified the gaps, fill them in. You need to make it easy for your followers to take action, to share your stories and to help you achieve your vision.
4 When you are giving instructions, use a story. It's much easier for people to remember instructions when they're presented in this framework.
5 Refine your story so it's simple. Keep paring back your story until it's succinct and easy to remember.
6 Don't let your story end. Keep people engaged with a new goal, a new idea, a new dream.

CHAPTER 9

Your media story

Picture this. Your business is featured on the cover of a national publication. You're invited onto the country's top-rating breakfast talk show, then you're asked to appear on a radio program. You feel like a rock star. You get tonnes of press coverage. Your website traffic goes through the roof and your phones are ringing off the hook. It's an entrepreneurial dream.

The right kind of media coverage can build your profile, bring in valuable customers and put your business on the map. But how do you achieve this media equivalent of the Holy Grail? How do you make yourself interesting enough to journalists and editors that they give you that coveted spot on the cover?

By telling the right stories.

That's right. Getting press coverage isn't a dark art that can be conjured up only by public relations agencies and spin doctors. To get press coverage for your business you need an understanding of what kind of stories the media want and how to provide them. This is worth getting right because media coverage is free. If you can get a journalist interested enough to write a story, you can end up with a page in a newspaper or magazine dedicated to your business, and unlike buying an advertisement, you didn't have to pay for it. If you don't have big bucks to splash around on a costly advertising campaign, getting free publicity can be one of the most cost-effective ways to promote your business.

The secret to telling the right stories to the media boils down to … tailoring. Pure and simple. Tailoring your story to specific media outlets. If you tell the same business story all the time, you're probably not going to have a high strike rate. The key is to focus on the specific elements of your story that would be particularly interesting to that publication, TV show or radio program.

You might be wondering, 'Why can't I just tell my story the way I've always told it and let the journalist pick out the bits they find interesting?' The reality is that journalists are busy. They are bombarded with hundreds of stories every day. And they won't know the nuances of your business story as intimately as you do, so they may simply miss some elements of your story that could be ideal for their publication. It's your responsibility to ensure that these elements are brought to their attention. Your business may be the most interesting enterprise in the world, but the journalist may not recognise it if you don't spell out *why* their readers or audience will find it relevant, interesting and useful.

The key here is to be able to provide them with a media release that covers exactly the topic they would want to write about. You'll get a better hit rate with a journalist if you get specific. Don't just provide them with general information about your company. Suggest an angle that will suit their particular publication or media outlet.

So the seventh power story in your arsenal is your Media Story. This story will be shaped differently depending on what kind of media you're talking to. It's a story that entrepreneur Matt Barrie has mastered over the past few years as CEO of Freelancer.com.

Matt's first challenge is describing what his website actually does. There's the long version, and then there's this one: 'We're eBay for jobs.' It's a succinct statement that encapsulates what Freelancer.com is all about. 'Employers' looking to outsource projects post details about the job on the site. These could range from website design and video editing to translating documents. Then freelancers from all over the world bid on the jobs. As an employer, you don't necessarily pick the lowest bid. You can review the online profile of the freelancer, which details their experience, examples of their work and ratings from previous employers, and select from any of the freelancers who bid on your job.

You don't have to be a big company to be an employer. Most employers are small business owners in the western world—from countries such as Australia, the US and the UK—who are looking for more cost-effective freelancers. Typically, these freelancers come from developing countries such as Bangladesh, the Philippines, India and Romania. And they are prepared to work at a fraction of the cost that business owners are used to paying. In fact, the average project on Freelancer.com is a mere $200.

'It's common to hear from Australian businesses who have been quoted $10 000 to $20 000 for a website design,' says Matt. 'They post the project on Freelancer.com and end up with a professionally designed site that costs $1000.'

While the old saying is 'When you pay peanuts, you get monkeys', Matt insists this isn't the case. 'Often, business owners say they get better service, quicker turnaround times, and even better designs from freelancers in the developing world. These freelancers fall over themselves to serve clients better because, in their country, the minimum wage is usually $100 to $200 a month. Now they have a chance to earn $1000 designing a website. They want you as a long-term customer so they're going out of their way to give you great customer service.'

But with such small amounts transacted through the website, how does the site make money? Freelancer.com charges a small fee (around 3 per cent of the value of the project) when the job is complete. For a $200 job, that's $6. To make serious money, it needs a serious number of users. Matt has built a site that works where the technology is infinitely scalable. For it to reach the heights of eBay, he's just waiting for the rest of the world to arrive.

Not that its 3.5 million users are anything to be sneezed at. However, it hasn't quite reached the likes of eBay's 106 million users or Facebook's 900 million. Compared with these online behemoths, Freelancer.com still has a long way to go. But Matt is quietly confident.

Catching his breath in a peaceful business lounge in New York, a stone's throw from the mayhem of Times Square, Matt has been on the road for weeks. He's just come from interviews with *The Wall*

Street Journal and *The New York Times*. A month before he graced the cover of one of Australia's most respected magazines, *Good Weekend*. If there's one thing he's mastered in recent times, it's telling the Freelancer.com story.

The aim of the game is to get as many people as he can to use his site. Because it's not just business owners who can benefit. Anyone can use the site to look for freelancers to perform any task. Like the mummy blogger who wants a new-look blog redesign. Or the accountant who needs some data entry done. Or the kid in Long Island, New York, who actually used the site to find a small army of people who would throw water balloons at his neighbour's house. But to do this, Matt needs more users. To convince 'employers' to sign up he needs to tell the right stories, and these stories aren't simply about how to find cheap labour.

As an increasingly media-savvy player, Matt knows it's important to tailor his message to specific media outlets. 'The great thing about telling the right stories is that it's then so much easier to land press coverage. And that's great for us because we need to have a large number of customers as we make a relatively small amount for each transaction. We need to get as much reach as possible.

'If I'm with a highbrow publication like *The New York Times* or *The Economist*, then I might focus on the macro story about disruption of global labour markets or what's going to happen in the long-term picture in western civilisation and developing economies,' says Matt. 'But we can drill that down. If I'm talking to a local newspaper in the Sydney suburb of Manly, I can provide them with a real example of a business in Manly that is successfully using our site to reduce their costs.'

In chapter 2 we explored the science behind why the story of the Entrepreneur's Journey is so powerful. Whether through analysis or instinct, Matt understands the power behind this story. 'It's about transformation,' says Matt. 'That's what people like to see — other small businesses transform because that's what they want for themselves as well. But they need to relate to it. So if I'm talking to a magazine for accountants, I'll find real examples of how accountants are using the site. If we take that to a fashion magazine, I'll show how fashion people are using it. No matter what publication I'm talking to I can find a case study those readers will relate to. It's more powerful when you do that because they think "Someone just like me has used this service. And it worked for them".'

Matt's own journey began in 2007 when he wanted to find someone to perform simple data entry tasks on a large spreadsheet. The work was mundane and repetitive, but it had to be done. He tried convincing his friend's younger brother to do the job in between studying at university and socialising. Even with the promise of $2000 payment, it never got done. Matt turned to the internet and found a group of workers in Vietnam who completed the task in three days—for the princely sum of $200. This is when the seed of the idea for Freelancer.com was planted. He knew there was an opportunity to connect people in the western world with those looking for work in the developing world. And it's this 'light bulb' story that Matt tells journalists when they ask about how the business was born.

Having been featured in publications all over the world, Matt has clearly figured out what the media want. So how can you do the same for your business? What should you do to share your story with the media?

How to share your story with the media

The most common way to share your story with the media is through a media release. Of course, you always have the option of calling journalists and talking to them about your business. But, more often than not, they'll still say, 'Send me a media release about it.'

What exactly is a media release?

Quite simply, a media (or press) release packages your story and delivers it in a form the media are familiar with. It is the means by which journalists and editors most often receive information about a product, event, business or project. It is usually a written document, and these days the most common method of distribution is via email.

Media releases conform to a typical structure—the inverted pyramid or upside-down triangle structure. This means it begins with the most important information, which is typically followed by information in descending order of importance so the least essential information is at the end of the release.

Why is it structured this way?

Media releases and news stories are structured this way—with the most important information at the top, then the rest of the information presented in order of decreasing importance—so even if people read only the first paragraphs, they will be presented with all the key facts. Another reason is that if a subeditor of the newspaper has to make the piece shorter, either to incorporate another breaking story or to make room for an advertisement, he or she can cut from the bottom in the knowledge that the most important information is retained. See figure 9.1.

Figure 9.1: the inverted pyramid

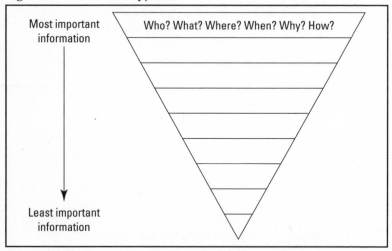

The inverted pyramid is the traditional structure of the news story. These are the stories that you typically read in the first few pages of the newspaper. With the most important facts placed at the top, you'll find the *who*, *what*, *where*, *when*, *why* and *how* in the first part of the story.

So let's say it's a news story about a new pet-friendly airline being launched in Australia. The first paragraph of the media release will contain the key information.

> Pet Lovers Airlines will enter the Australian aviation market tomorrow when its maiden flight takes off from Sydney Airport at 10 am

heading to Melbourne. Passengers on the flight include: Lester the Jack Russell, Rambo the chihuahua cross, Rex the pure-bred Australian Tiffanie cat, and Rocky the long-haired burmilla cat. They will all fly inside the cabin seated next to their owners to minimise trauma to the animals when flying in the cargo hold. In an Australian first, the national carrier will sell seats for pets weighing up to 20 kg to all capital cities.

Who? Pet Lovers Airlines.
What? A pet-friendly airline.
Where? Maiden flight from Sydney to Melbourne. National carrier servicing all capital cities.
When? Launched tomorrow.
Why? To minimise trauma to the animals when flying in the cargo hold.
How? Pets are seated in the cabin next to their owners.

The rest of the release is then likely to consist of:

* supplementary details
* background information
* quotes from key spokespeople.

So the ensuing paragraphs might look like this:

The brainchild of pet-lover and billionaire Jack Johnson, the airline's headquarters and fleet are based in Sydney. However, it will fly to a total of 15 destinations in Australia and plans to expand to New Zealand next year. 'It's time for Australian airlines to enter the 21st century,' said Johnson. 'These days, pets are part of the family. They shouldn't have to sit in a cold, dark cargo hold all alone. Some animals are terrified. I've always believed that pets should be able to travel with their owners in plane cabins. I got sick of waiting for Australian airlines to allow this, so I decided to do something about it.'

An entrepreneur and investor, Johnson had several companies in the transport industry including a freight forwarding business and a rail logistics company. Although this is his first foray into aviation, Johnson says he is confident in his new venture and expects to capture 20 per cent of the market within two years. 'We've partnered with the best aviation brains in the world,' said Johnson. 'Our utmost commitment is to the safety of our passengers—humans AND pets. Not only have we complied with every safety standard required by regulators, in most cases we've exceeded what's been asked for.'

President of Petcare Australia Sue Smith said: 'We've tested the experience on Pet Lovers Airlines and believe this is a much better alternative than what's being offered by other airlines. This is a huge step forward in the way we treat our pets. Some pets are traumatised when they have to travel in the cargo hold and have to be sedated, which is not ideal.'

Pets have been allowed to travel in airline cabins in the US and Europe for many years. On Pet Lovers Airlines, all pets will need to wear a safety harness during the flight. However, pets are encouraged not to operate mobile devices at any time. The airline provides special pet meals (on request) and has designated 'pet-relieving' bathrooms. For more information contact:

Michael Miller, Public Relations Manager
Pet Lovers Airlines
Email: michael@petloversairlines.com
Ph: (02) 5555 1111
www.PetLoversAirlines.com

Look for opportunities for good story angles

You need to give a journalist a *reason* for writing about your business today. You can't just rely on your own belief that you've created the best thing since sliced bread. That's not going to cut it. In most cases, a journalist needs a topical reason to run a story on you. Consider these angles:

Seasonal

Can you tie your story to a seasonal event. For example, every January media outlets all over the world run stories about how to keep new year's resolutions. When winter is approaching, there are stories on how to ward off the flu. Summer produces stories about staying safe in the sun and how to entertain kids during school holidays.

Think about how you can tie your business to a seasonal event. Let's say you're a professional organiser (often used to de-clutter homes and provide concierge services such as ordering the weekly groceries). You might comment that every spring you see a 30 per cent increase in bookings as people come out of hibernation and are keen to de-clutter: 'It happens every year like clockwork. People get energised—it's like they get a new lease on life. I've also noticed a trend that people are using this time not only to clean out their home, but also to sort out their relationships. Now half my spring bookings are people who want me to help them split from their spouse and start a new life.'

Event-related

Peg your story to an upcoming event. Let's say you're a florist. February could be an ideal time to talk about how Valentine's Day flowers have changed over the past decade: 'Two years ago, every arrangement had roses and baby's breath. Now, no customer wants to be caught dead sending baby's breath. These days it's hip to send Australian wildflowers.'

Awards

Have you won any major business awards? This is an ideal angle when seeking media coverage. The biggest mistake I see business owners make when they win an award is to delay telling the media until weeks, sometimes months, after the announcement. By then it's simply old news.

If you're a finalist for an award, I strongly recommend that you take the bold step of writing a media release in preparation for winning. I know that some business owners will consider this as either incredibly arrogant or likely to jinx their chances. But it's simply smart and strategic. Trust me, you want to be ready to go when the big announcement is made. You don't want to be crafting this the morning after a gala awards event where you've been celebrating with your team into the wee hours. If you don't win, simply don't send it out and no-one will be any the wiser.

Trends and survey results

If you've noticed any significant trends in your industry, community or business, this might be a good story angle for the media. Let's say you're a body corporate strata manager and you've noticed that an increasing number of cars are being illegally dumped in the parking areas of the apartment buildings you manage. If there has been a big rise compared with five years ago, this could be a trend worth discussing. If you're a recruitment company and you've noticed a sustained increase in the number of CEOs entering the market as a result of layoffs, this is definitely a story angle.

Perhaps you undertake customer surveys or can access results from industry association studies. If survey results reveal significant trends or depict an interesting snapshot of society, can you provide the media with a good angle by constructing a relevant story from it. For example: 'Our customer survey shows that 80 per cent of consumers chose their smartphone as their main means of communication in 2007, but in 2012 it's their tablet. Our customers, who are typically over 45, tell us they prefer emailing on the tablet, with its bigger screen area, than SMSing or talking on the phone.'

The importance of statistics

We've discussed how statistics shouldn't dominate your passion story or your business story. They are vital to your media story, however, or at least your media release.

Journalists love statistics! They simply can't base a story on the idea that 'our sales are huge' or 'the traffic to our website has skyrocketed' or 'the market for this widget is massive'. Although they need an engaging story, they also need facts that are grounded in objective reality. Statistics add credibility to your story, as shown in table 9.1.

Table 9.1: use of statistics in your media release

NO	YES
'Our sales are massive.'	'Our sales have consistently increased by 40 per cent each year since 2007.'
'The traffic to our website has skyrocketed.'	'Last year we averaged about 3000 unique visitors a month. Now it's closer to 3000 unique visitors *a day*.'
'The market for this widget is huge.'	'We expect to capture 25 per cent of the market by the end of the year. And our forecast is that we'll take 50 per cent of market share within three years.'
'We're thrilled with the number of downloads of our app on iTunes.'	'Our app is downloaded about 500 times a day. It spiked to 7500 downloads when we appeared on the *Today Show*.'

Smart ways to create stories

If you're scratching your head for a story angle that you think the media might be interested in, consider this: you don't have to wait around for a newsworthy incident to occur. Why not create one?

Let's revisit Matt Barrie. With the wealth of stories at his fingertips, Matt still understands the power of creating stories. If you want to be a master storyteller, you can't tell the same story all the time. You need fresh material, and it's got to be interesting. But you can't just sit around waiting for good stories to appear. One of the best ways to elicit fresh material is to provide a structured framework for stories to flourish.

Freelancer.com did this successfully in 2012 when it ran the contest 'Expose the Freelancer.com logo', calling on people to send in innovative videos showing how they gained exposure for the site's logo. What started as a fun way to involve its community—with $25 000 worth of prize money—resulted in media coverage and attention worth a hundred times that. And an endless resource of stories that Matt can now use in keynote presentations, interviews and other marketing initiatives. While using a contest to promote the site's logo may sound like a cheap way to get advertising, it's the people and stories that entered the logo contest that have proven to be the heroes here.

Like Freelancer.com user Stephen Karigo from the US, who got permission from the US Federal Aviation Administration to fly over New York's air space towing a 10 × 45 foot banner of the Freelancer.com logo over Long Island, Manhattan, New Jersey, Ellis Island and the iconic Statue of Liberty. Or Gorakh Nath Timilsina from Nepal who hung a 10 × 50 foot banner for an entire day from Bhimsen Tower, the tallest tower in Nepal. The entries ranged from the sublime to the crazy. One keen entrant took the Freelancer.com logo and swam with sharks; four skydivers jumped out of a plane flying a Freelancer.com banner; and another built a spaceship-like flying object complete with Freelancer.com logo, bamboozling local residents and television stations who saw it in the night sky, and landing a mention on NBC's *Today Show*.

It's stories like these that get media time. Even more importantly, they are shared via social media. As all entries were submitted via YouTube, they were immediately shareable at the click of a mouse, with some entries attracting tens of thousands of 'likes' on Facebook. Of course, these stories gain significant attention when they are first released. But even after the first wave of viewers dies down, they continue life on the internet, reaching new audiences as time passes.

Unlike a news story in the traditional media, which becomes tomorrow's fish and chip wrapping or disappears into the vault of a television studio, you can leverage the power of storytelling by getting your story online and sharing it through social media. But more on that later.

Matt describes sharing through social media in developing countries as word-of-mouth on steroids. In addition to the traditional media mentions of the abovementioned logo stunts, people could vote for their favourite one by 'liking' it on Facebook. This automatically featured on their news feeds, spreading the word to their friends and followers.

In an auditorium at the Austin Convention Center in Texas, Matt is a featured speaker at the South by South West Interactive Festival in 2012. He's rattling off the statistics behind Freelancer.com. 'We have 3.5 million users and 1.5 million projects,' he says. 'The internet is in the middle of delivering the next big tectonic shift to society. The global labour markets are disrupted. There are 7 billion people in the world, but only 2 billion are on the internet. That means that 5 billion people — or 70 per cent of the world's population — are not. But they're coming now. And they want a job.'

I get it. The numbers are big. My brain computes that there's a lot of opportunity. But even though these numbers are truly massive, it's the story of Nazma Rahman from Bangladesh that brings it home. After Matt's presentation in Austin, he shows me Nazma's video entry in the competition. What starts as a handful of Bangladeshis milling around a 2000 square foot billboard of the Freelancer.com logo grows into a larger crowd of people. The women are in traditional dress, their saris topped with Freelancer.com T-shirts. The men wear the same t-shirt. On closer inspection, I see they each also carry the logo emblazoned on headbands, flags and balloons. The throng starts marching but grows into a 3000-strong army, who eventually congregate in a dusty square in the rural town of Chapainawabganj. There Nazma has organised banners that advertise Freelancer.com's services, and has set up a bank of computers to demonstrate how the site works.

Even Matt seems to find this a tad surreal. 'When I first saw it, I thought it was pretty amazing to see them marching through the streets,' he says. 'Then I realised: oh my God, they've printed 3000 T-shirts with our logo. Then I saw the little headbands and realised they were all waving flags with Freelancer on them.' He shakes his head in disbelief. 'It's makes the hairs on the back of your neck stand up.'

When Matt was in the Philippines, he appeared on a half-hour television segment, alongside two local freelancers. 'The presenter interviewing us was a glamorous woman and she asks the freelancers: 'So you're a web developer, and you're a stay-at-home mother. Do you supplement what you do in your daily lives with a bit of money on the side using Freelancer?'

'One of our freelancers said: "Oh no, we make a lot more money freelancing than we do at our full-time jobs!" You could see the presenter was trying to understand how this was possible. By the end of the segment, she gives me her business card and asks: "Are there opportunities for voiceover experts on this site?"'

Ultimately, Matt has realised, the best way to leverage the power of storytelling is to understand that you don't have to be the only storyteller. 'When people have a good experience, they tell everyone else a story about it,' he says.

Media alerts and callout services

Pitching to journalists is one way to get your story into the media. You should also sign up for media alert or 'callout' services. Journalists use these services when they are looking for specific case studies, experts and people to interview. You sign up for free emails that feature a list of the types of experts, case studies or sources that journalists are looking for to comment on topics they are writing about. One Australian-based media callout service is <www.sourcebottle.com.au>. A similar service in the US is <www.reporterconnection.com>. The key to success with services such as Sourcebottle and Reporter Connection is ensuring that you provide the information journalists ask for. Let's say a journalist is looking for 'an expert who can comment on the current food crisis in Australia'. This kind of response is not going to get you very far:

'I am an expert and I can provide comment on this.'

It communicates nothing about your expertise or why you would be ideal to comment on the topic. Instead, you might try something like this:

> I am a food economist based in Sydney. I have strong views on the current food crisis in Australia based on my research into imported versus locally produced foods, particularly fruit. If you would like specific comment on how the recent Queensland floods have affected the food crisis, I can also expand on that. I'm happy to talk any time this week. My phone number is...

If you're an established business, you might use the services of a public relations agency to get publicity for your product, service or business. After all, that's probably not your core expertise, so it makes sense for you to outsource this job to the experts. However, if you're starting out and you aren't flush with cash, you might not be able to afford one. If that's the case, media alerts and callouts can be a useful resource. But you also need to understand how to approach journalists and editors. You'll find fundamental guidelines on dealing with the media in the exclusive resources section at <www.powerstoriesbook.com>.

Photography

You've heard that a picture is worth a thousand words, and this is particularly true when it comes to the media. Never underestimate the power of a good photograph. Of course, some media outlets have the time and resources to send their own photographer, but these days many don't. So you should ensure that you have a selection of decent photos that you can supply to the media if they need them. You don't have to commission Annie Leibowitz. You just need a few decent shots in which you're not drunk, holding your baby or dressed in taffeta as a bridesmaid at your sister's wedding.

A photo can be critical to how much coverage you get. If you think I'm being dramatic here, I'm not. If you have a great, professionally taken photo, you could end up with a full page (or even the cover) of some magazines. But if you send that photo you took last time you were in Bali and ask the journalist to crop your kids out, then don't expect to get too many column inches in their publication. And also don't expect them to call you back too soon.

I know there are photo-shy people who believe their story should stand on its own merits. But in reality, all other things being equal, if a media outlet has the choice of using a great photo supplied by your competitor versus the fuzzy one supplied by you, which one are they going to choose?

It's all in the timing

Journalists work to deadlines. If they have called you back to get more information about your product or service, chances are they are close to their deadline for your story. So return their calls or emails as soon as possible—within an hour is ideal. If you really can't postpone what you're doing—say you're in a meeting or at a wedding—then try to sneak out to make a quick call just to say: 'I'm at a meeting/wedding and I can't talk right now, but I can call you in two hours. Does that work for you?'

Generally, this will be acceptable. Journalists need to know you are going to get back to them. It takes the pressure off them, because if they don't know whether or not you've even got their message, then they will start looking for another source. If they find someone else to talk to in the meantime, you may have lost this opportunity for publicity. Even if you call back later, they are unlikely to quote you in the story if they already have what they need from the other source.

I sometimes shake my head at the things people do. Like the business owner who sent me a media release and then went on vacation, refusing to take calls to be interviewed. Needless to say, I didn't write about him. I wasn't being petulant about it—I simply had a deadline.

Blogger outreach

It's not just journalists and traditional media who can give vast exposure to your brand. With the blogosphere growing at a rate of knots, bloggers are becoming increasingly influential. Certain bloggers have bigger communities than some traditional media outlets. But since the barriers to entry are zero in the blogging world (you can set up a blog for free within minutes), there is an entire spectrum of bloggers out there, ranging from complete novices with no readers (except maybe their mother and their cat) to popular bloggers who have armies of followers hanging on their every word.

Just as in the traditional media, you want to target your messages to bloggers who reach the same or a similar audience to yours. There's no point reaching out to, say, tech bloggers—no matter how big their readership—if a tech-savvy audience is not your objective.

The key is to find influential bloggers who:

- reach an audience of your target customers
- write about topics and issues that are in sync with your products/services.

Compared with traditional media, which have been around more or less in their current form for decades, the blogosphere is still relatively young. So while there are clear guidelines on how to approach traditional media, the rules are still being written on what's known as 'blogger outreach'—that is, the process of engaging bloggers with your product, service or brand, in the hope they will spread the word by blogging about them. This can take the form of product giveaways, sponsored posts, straightforward advertising, product reviews and so on.

The confusing part is that every blogger is different. Some expect payment to write about your product or service (particularly if they have a huge audience), while others are more than happy to talk about it at no cost as long as it's relevant to their readers.

In other words, the editorial policies of today's bloggers vary widely. This variation is likely to be rationalised over the next few years to a more standard approach. In the meantime, many bloggers agree that when payment is involved—either through free product, advertising or a paid post—this should be disclosed. Indeed, in the US this disclosure is required by the Federal Trade Commission.

So what kind of story should you be telling bloggers? You approach this in a similar way to your media story. After all, bloggers are part of a growing cohort of influential leaders in the social media space. You need to tailor your message to suit the audience of that particular blog, and the personality of that particularly blogger.

The blogosphere is constantly evolving. One way to find bloggers and social media influencers who would be interested in writing about your product or business is via a callout service like <www.SocialCallout.com>, in which I'm an investor. If you're new to the blogging world, you can find more guidelines about this and how to make the most out of your relationship with bloggers in the exclusive resources section at <www.powerstoriesbook.com>.

Your actions

Your media story

Ultimately, your media story is not just one story that you tell again and again, hoping it will stick. To make your story truly work, you need a strategic approach. To create effective media stories, you should set aside a couple of hours to brainstorm angles, identify the right media and craft a tailored message to suit.

Follow these steps or download your Media Story template in the exclusive resources section at <www.powerstoriesbook.com>.

1 Define the audience you want to reach.
2 Determine the traditional and social media they read, listen to or watch.
3 Analyse the types of stories featured by this media source.
4 Tailor your story to this media source.
5 Determine an angle that will give journalists a reason to run it.
6 Distribute your story via a media release.
7 Create opportunities to develop newsworthy stories.

CHAPTER 10

From storytelling to story sharing

You can't help but notice Kyle Maynard. He's good looking, charismatic and has pretty impressive pecs. This 25-year-old entrepreneur combines a successful speaking career with a business that fulfils one of his greatest passions, fitness. When Kyle is not on the road to and from speaking engagements, he is running his own CrossFit gym, which he founded in 2008 in Suwanee, Georgia, in the US. He has also written *The New York Times* best-selling book *No Excuses*, been inducted in the US National Wrestling Hall of Fame, broken world records in weightlifting, competed in mixed martial arts, and been a guest on *Oprah*, *Larry King* and several other top-rating television shows. He's even been a model for Abercrombie & Fitch, snapped by none other than the late legendary photographer Bruce Weber, who also shot him for *Vanity Fair*.

So when I find myself sitting across from Kyle during lunch at a conference we're both attending in August 2011, I sure as hell don't compare notes with him about my sporting achievements (or complete lack thereof). We grab food from the poolside buffet before navigating our way to the tables set aside for conference attendees. Like many fit young guys, he's laden his plate with what seems to me like in inordinate amount of protein but skipped the dessert selection.

Over grilled chicken, refried beans and salad, I learned Kyle's story. Born in 1986 with a condition known as congenital amputation, Kyle's arms end above his elbows and his legs end mid thigh. He has no hands or feet. However, this hasn't stopped him from living a normal life. 'That's what my parents wanted for me,' says Kyle. 'That's what I wanted for myself.'

Kyle gets around without any assistance except for a wheelchair, which he seems to jump from, and fold and stash in one deft move. He lives on his own in a three-storey townhouse, with his bedroom on the third floor, and leads a regular life. Kyle drives, types at 50 words per minute on his computer or iPad and runs his business, just like anyone else. He always shunned prosthetic limbs for himself because he felt they limited his ability to get around.

His parents made a decision very early on to treat him like a normal, healthy boy. Kyle went to school, played football, joined the wrestling team, and lived with his parents and three sisters, who were not born with the condition. At school, in his first year of wrestling he was beaten 35 times in a row. It's a losing streak that would make anyone feel hopeless. To top it off, Kyle had to listen to the naysayers. 'People would tell me that I'd never win a match,' he says. 'I'd overhear conversations where other people would say that what I was trying to do was completely impossible.'

His parents didn't want him to quit, but he sure as hell didn't want to sign up again the following year. 'My dad kept asking me if I was going to wrestle again and I avoided the conversation like the plague,' says Kyle. 'I didn't want to do it, but then my dad told me that he didn't win a match his entire first season, and that he became a very successful college wrestler. So I believed him—and I signed up. I figured if he could do that, then I could too.'

Kyle went on to win 36 matches in his final year of high school, defeating several state champions. He was ranked twelfth in his weight class at the national championships. And in case you're wondering if this was a special category, it wasn't. Kyle competed head to head with able-bodied wrestlers.

'It wasn't until years later that I found out my dad blatantly lied to me about losing all those matches when he was at school. He did that to try to get me to sign up to wrestling again. I was shocked. But, you know, it worked.'

It seems a natural extension that Kyle then embraced the world of mixed martial arts, or cage fighting. But he hit a wall in 2007 when the Georgia Athletic and Entertainment Commission refused to give him a licence to compete. 'That left me without much choice but to fight in Alabama, where there was no commission to stop it,' says Kyle, who eventually competed in 2009.

Although he got his opportunity to fight, he also attracted the haters. 'People posted nasty things online and on YouTube. Some said I was going to be the first televised death in the sport. People would email me saying that if they were fighting me they wouldn't have a problem kicking my skull in. One guy even said: "Come take a chainsaw and cut off my arms and legs so that I can get on *Oprah* like Kyle."

'I felt sorry for those people. For me, the experience was worth having. It was one of the most amazing experiences of my life.' Kyle's journey was captured in the film documentary 'A Fighting Chance'.

Now sitting by the pool in the warm California sun, Kyle seems more businessman than cage fighter. Only his pecs give him away.

Make your story relate to others

Seven months after that conference, I reconnect with Kyle. He's in Phoenix, Arizona, for a speaking gig and this time when we chat he's eating French fries. We fill each other in on what we've been up to. I've been working, doing a bit of travelling and renovating a house. You know, normal things. Kyle, on the other hand, has climbed Mount Kilimanjaro. Yes, you read that correctly. He climbed 5895 metres (19 341 feet) to the summit of Africa's highest mountain—and he crawled the whole way.

Despite Kyle's desire to live a 'normal' life, no-one would argue that he's lived an extraordinary one so far. So it's no wonder he's in demand as a speaker, spending half the year travelling, sharing his story. 'The most important thing about storytelling is to realise that the story we tell, even if it's our own story—it's not actually about us. My story is just a metaphor to help other people. It's about being able to make your story relate to others and tie into their own experiences. It's about making an impact on someone else's life. To me, that's exciting.'

Kyle wasn't always so passionate about sharing his story, however. 'I used to treat it like a job. It was a career. It wasn't a passion,' he says. 'A few years ago, I was burnt out from speaking. I was depressed and I was ready to quit.'

It was a chance encounter in the departure lounge of an airport in North Carolina that became a turning point for Kyle. 'I saw two guys who kept looking at me so I decided to reach out to them and say hi,' says Kyle. 'I jumped in my wheelchair and wheeled myself over. I reached out to shake the first one's hand and saw that it had been almost completely burnt off. I saw that he had burns all up his arm and that his friend had terrible burns on the side of his own body. Then they told me their story.

'They had been in the army military police guarding a convoy. They were in a fuel truck, so it was full of gasoline, and it was hit with a rocket. Fire came up over the dashboard and burned the first guy's hands. His friend jumped on him to try to extinguish the flames, but that burned the side of his body so severely that even his kids couldn't recognise him.

'So they were lying in their hospital beds in San Antonio, Texas. They wouldn't speak to any of the hospital staff, doctors or nurses. They wouldn't even return calls to their family. They would only speak to each other. They said that on the seventh day, lying in bed, they made a suicide pact that they would take each other's lives. On that day they saw my story on HBO, and that's what got them to stop.

'They helped me find my purpose. They helped me find my belief in why I share my story. These days, I'll encounter people who heard my story three or four years ago. And they'll come up to me and tell me how that story changed their life. It still kind of takes my breath away.'

'My story isn't so epic'

There is no doubt that Kyle's story is an epic one. And most of us don't have tales of cage fighting or dramatic ascents up Kilimanjaro with which to regale our friends. However, Kyle emphasises that your stories don't have to be epic to have an impact. 'They just need to be yours,' he says. 'Truly your own. Because that is so much more powerful than telling someone else's story. And often it's the stories about everyday incidents, like going to the grocery store or getting dressed, that have more power than the ones about cage fighting or mountain climbing.'

Kyle shares his story not only through his keynote speeches, but also on his blog at <www.kyle-maynard.com>, Twitter, Facebook and videos on YouTube, and in his book. When people are inspired by Kyle, they can continue to connect with him online, to follow his story.

To me, this is the cornerstone of story sharing in today's digital world. Of course nothing can beat connecting with someone in person—either through a one-on-one conversation like my poolside chat with Kyle or at a speaking gig—but there's only 24 hours in a day, and only one of you. The most efficient way to share your story widely is through online social media.

Before you start sharing ...

Before you even begin sharing your stories online, it's important to start listening. You know that guy who walks into the conversation you're having at a barbecue and starts telling his stories while other people are still in the middle of theirs. You don't want to be that guy. Or the woman at a networking event who barges in on your conversation and thinks that's okay as long as she opens with 'I'm so sorry, I don't mean to interrupt but ... ', then she proceeds to tell you about how her business can help you with pay-per-click advertising. And, here you go, here's a flyer for the special offer she's got on this week. But sorry, she has to rush off because her husband's waiting in the car.

These people never bother to listen because they are too busy broadcasting their own messages. Just as in real-life social settings, people don't respond well if your approach is all about ... you.

I know an entrepreneur (we'll call her Kathie) who communicates with her database only when she wants to sell them something. 'I'm just going to do an email blast,' she says. When she's on Twitter she only tweets about her products and never bothers replying to any of her followers. Her Facebook page is dominated by links to her blog posts or reviews of her book, and when people comment, she doesn't respond.

I sometimes wonder if she's trying to dig her business into an early grave. Kathie simply sees social media as a channel to broadcast information instead of a way to have a conversation. And that means she's missing out on valuable opportunities to find out what people think about her products, or to get ideas on those she might introduce in the future. It drives me nuts and I want to shake her.

I secretly think Kathie wants to appear a bit like a rock star. She believes that if she cultivates an air of inaccessibility, this will make other people think she's too successful or busy to bother with trivialities like social interaction. She doesn't seem to realise that this aloof approach just makes her seem like a jerk. You don't want to be a social media tosser like Kathie. So when it comes to learning about listening, it's worth getting lessons from some masters.

Determining your customers' needs

I've walked onto the set of *WarGames*. Well, at least that's what it feels like to me. If you're not familiar with this iconic 1983 movie starring Matthew Broderick, it's about a teenage computer hacker who unwittingly breaks into a US Defense Department computer system and almost starts a global nuclear war.

I'll confess. I loved this movie. It started a fascination with technology that I have to this day. The movie's climactic scenes are set in the headquarters of NORAD (North American Aerospace Defense Command) built deep within the Colorado mountains. Massive screens dominate the control centre, towering over ranks of grim military personnel, each with their own screen and control panels. Operators wearing headsets watch the huge screens above them, which offer a bird's-eye view of the global thermonuclear warfare that's about to unfold. There's a direct phone line to the President of the United States.

'Flush the bombers. Get the subs in launch mode. We are at DEFCON 1,' intones the much-decorated general with the gravitas of someone who knows that millions of lives are in his hands.

In the cavernous room I'm standing in now, the man at the front has the same kind of military solemnity. With his feet planted squarely, he surveys the room and speaks clearly to the assembled visitors. He has a crew-cut, wears an immaculately pressed shirt and peppers his explanations with words like 'deployed', 'assets', 'political situation', 'disaster' and 'logistics'. The room looks like a Hollywood movie set. I half expect Matthew Broderick to walk around the corner.

But this is not global thermonuclear war. It's the Dell Global Command Center in Round Rock, Texas, and the assets they are deploying aren't intercontinental ballistic missiles, but Dell computers. It's hard to suppress a giggle when the speaker gravely explains how Dell uses state-of-the-art tools to predict the path of hurricanes so it can reroute delivery of computers or parts to get them to the customer on time. Through a complex tracking system they can determine the parts depot closest to the customer, gauge the capacity of its logistics partners (such as courier companies) and use this information to ensure it meets that customer's expectations as per their specific service level agreement.

This is all represented visually on the massive screens at the front of the room, which feature Google Earth images that can be zoomed in to street level, and plot information on the speed of traffic for some areas—certain hotspots have real-time camera views.

'If there's a meeting of political leaders, we know the streets that will be shut down. This can cause delays for hours. So we determine alternative plans for fulfilment,' he continues. Dell's seemingly omniscient command centre tracks weather, world events, even power outages. 'During a recent incident in New York, half the city shut down. We had to put assets on helicopters to make sure they got to their destination on time.'

This military approach to logistics and operations is unsurprising when you consider that Dell delivers an ever growing number of computers around the world each year. In the fiscal year ending 2011, Dell's revenue was US$62.12 billion. It has 109 000 team members globally. That's big.

When you're dealing with this kind of volume, the global chatter about your brand, whether it's good, bad or ugly, can be deafening. But how do you eavesdrop on these conversations? How do you know when someone is saying wonderful things about you (so you can thank them) or slagging you off as the worst experience of their life (so you can hopefully fix the problems)? While you're never going to be able to eavesdrop on a private conversation two people are having over coffee, you can certainly listen to the online conversations, and that's increasingly where people are sharing their opinions on product, service and customer experiences.

They're checking in on Facebook or Foursquare with a photo of the delicious restaurant meal they just ordered. They're tweeting about how much they love (or hate) their new smartphone. They're writing reviews on their blogs about everything from gadgets and wine to books and TV shows. They're bitching about your customer service on online forums or raving about how good it is on Yelp. Whether you are a behemoth like Dell or a small business owner, the challenges are the same. It's actually harder for a company with volumes like Dell to keep up with all the conversations in the social space than it is for a more nimble small business with a more manageable number of interactions.

So where do you start?

According to Richard Binhammer, a director on Dell's social media and community team, it starts with listening. That's exactly what he did when he began focusing on Dell's social media presence back in 2006. Richard makes the point that conversations about you are happening whether you are a part of them or not.

You may think that your profile is nowhere near as big as Dell or that as a relatively new business you don't have anything to listen to yet. While that might be true, it's worth using the right tools to check, just in case there are conversations about you or your products you didn't know were happening. Even if you're convinced that no-one is talking about you, you should still be listening to the kinds of conversations that are going on about your competitors or the types of products in your space.

'You absolutely want to know about the conversations that are going on,' says Richard, standing outside Dell's Social Media Listening Command Center. Located in another part of the company's Round Rock head office, this is a scaled-down version of the *WarGames*-style room that oversees the logistics and 'deployment of assets'.

The screens in the social media command centre don't feature street-view images of traffic hubs or track the location of Dell delivery vehicles. Instead, the graphics represent customer sentiment about Dell. On one giant world map, green dots indicate the positive online mentions of Dell, measured by key words such as 'great experience' or 'Dell rocks' or 'Love my new Dell'. The red dots indicate the locations in the world where someone is posting a negative comment, measured by key words such as 'Dell sucks'.

It's no surprise that Richard understands the power of public opinion. Now based in Texas, he comes from Canada, where he worked on the Prime Minister's national campaign, before moving into public affairs and corporate communications in the US.

On the day of my visit, the customer sentiment screen happens to be dominated by green. However, this hasn't always been the case. Back in 2005, Dell was getting less than stellar reports on various blogs, with negative reports on both products and customer support. These experiences weren't just reported, they were shared, with other unhappy customers joining in the conversation. But how do you fix these issues if you don't hear about them? What if the conversations are going on around you but you don't have the radar to pick them up?

These days there are many social media management and reporting tools. They start from basic free tools such as Google Alerts, which alerts you whenever your chosen key word (such as the name of your company or product) is mentioned. More complex ones, such as monitoring and engagement tool Radian6 (used by Dell), can provide more sophisticated analytics and reporting.

'In the past, people's perspective of a product or brand often relied on traditional fact-based reporting, like you would find on news sites, in advertising or from industry commentators,' says Richard. 'With social media, this has shifted profoundly to perspectives that are more subjective. In a sense, they are crowd sourced. And they're very powerful.'

This means that these days consumers are increasingly using recommendations from friends and user reviews (such as the book reviews on Amazon or restaurant review sites). It's not just the experts who are being relied on for opinions. Previously, food critics would review eateries and public opinion would be swayed by their verdict. Now you don't have to be a foodie to write about whether you had a good experience or not. If there are enough bad reviews from regular pundits, this has an impact on the way an eatery is viewed.

'In some cases, a single blog post can have as much power as a major news story,' says Richard. 'These days, people are publishers and they can influence opinion, especially if their messages are shared within their community. It's so much easier to share information online than ever before. So entire communities can form that can shape debates and impact on people's perceptions about a product.'

These communities can be anything from mummy blogging networks to small business groups. There are also those with niche interests that range from fans of *The Hunger Games* and car enthusiasts to digital photo devotees and people who make crafts out of cat hair. Yes, there really are communities of people who make crafts. With hair that falls out of their cats.

Richard says: 'If a conversation happens around a water cooler in Brisbane, Australia, about a Dell product, I have no idea it's going on. And it's very unlikely that it will be reported to me. But if that conversation happens on Facebook, in the blogosphere or on Twitter, not only can I learn from it, I can also engage and, if possible, fix any problems.

'It boils down to forming relationships. I've long stopped thinking of social media as a channel. It's a tool, like phone or email. Any business that is a smart business needs to be listening and engaging online.'

It's easy simply to assume that Dell has the budget, tools and resources to manage its social media, but it's important to note that Richard started this journey before many social media tools were even invented. 'Back in 2005, we didn't have Radian6 or the Social Media Listening Command Center,' he says. 'I was doing keyword searching—both for Dell and our industry—and set up Google blog alerts in order to see what was being said about us online. I'd copy all that into an Excel spreadsheet and work my way through it every day.'

Even for a company as huge as Dell, which is now mentioned on social media about 25 000 times every day, it started as a manual process. But now there's a range of low-cost or no-cost tools to help you do this from a single screen. If you're starting out, and you want tools to help you listen to what people are saying about your company, brand or product, you can find out more in the exclusive resources section at <www.powerstoriesbook.com>.

Which social media platforms?

If you hoped this book was going to offer a comprehensive directory of social media platforms, complete with instructions on how to share your stories on each one, it's not. That's simply because there are increasing numbers of social media platforms entering and exiting the online space. What's hot now may fade away next month, and it doesn't take long for a new social media darling to emerge. Instead, I'm going to suggest some practical examples of how to share your stories on a few of the key platforms, such as Twitter, Facebook, Pinterest, LinkedIn, blogs and Instagram. You can apply the same principles regardless of which social media app pops up to become the Next Big Thing.

Example 1: Sydney Writers' Centre

Customer story	Sydney Writers' Centre student John Smith becomes a published writer after completing our courses.
Blog	Write a post interviewing former student John Smith on how he transitioned from his old career as an architect to his new one as a full-time writer. Highlight the courses he's done and the steps he had to take to make it happen. Include how he came up with the inspiration for his latest sci-fi fantasy series.
Twitter	'Congratulations to our student John Smith for landing a three-book deal to publish his sci-fi fantasy series.' *[add link to the above blog post]*
Facebook	*[Upload a photo of the book's cover]* 'Check out our student John Smith's latest sci-fi fantasy book. Have you read it? What did you think?'

Example 2: Accounting firm

Business story	You're an accountant specialising in fast-growth small to medium-sized businesses that benefit from comprehensive tax planning.
Blog	Write a blog post on how businesses can access credit to fund high growth when the bank has already turned them away.
Twitter	Tweet alerts to remind people of key tax deadlines.
LinkedIn	On your LinkedIn status, share links to useful articles or resources about fast-growth businesses or reducing tax.

Example 3: ABC coffee machines

Product story	The new portable ABC coffee machines use only fair trade coffee and come in a range of fashionable colours.
Pinterest	Pin images for ABC coffee machines in various kitchens so potential customers can see how stylish they look 'in situ'.
Blog	Write regular posts on the farmers in Peru from whom this fair trade coffee is sourced. Each month you could profile one farmer and the story of how he has been able to lift his family out of poverty.
YouTube	How-to videos on how to use the machine.

Of course these examples are not exhaustive. There are countless other ways you can share your story. The key is to not get bogged down with this exercise. If you're spending half an hour crafting a tweet, you're not using your time wisely. You don't need to ponder every word. When it comes to short status updates on Twitter or Facebook, remind yourself that you're having a conversation and follow the same principles: be polite, respectful and helpful, but don't overthink it.

'It's all too much!'

If you've embraced social media, then you already know how you can share your stories using these channels. But if you're new to social media, the task may seem overwhelming. Trust me, using social media is one of the easiest activities to master. Anyone can do it. You just need to get started.

The *hard* work is in identifying and defining the right power stories you should be telling to grow your business. Hopefully, you've already learned how to do this for seven of your power stories. The *easy* work is to share these stories! Most of it can be done with the click of a mouse or a tap on your mobile device.

Here are the two excuses for inaction I hear most often:

- I don't have the time.
- I'm a private person. I don't want to share my life online.

So let's tackle these two excuses in turn.

'I don't have the time'

Okay, then don't share your stories, and don't experience how powerful it can be to do this. Fine? Let's move on then.

No, seriously, the reality is that you don't have to embrace social media. If you hate Facebook, don't want to spend time on Twitter and barely check your LinkedIn account, that's fine. You can still use your power stories. It's just that you'll be limiting how many people you can reach. And if you rely on traditional methods of sharing your story — networking, brochures, posters and so on — you need to understand that these methods are accounting for a smaller and smaller part of the marketing pie. So while your story will still reach people, there will be far more people you *won't* reach if you choose to ignore online channels and social media.

Recently a woman approached me at an event where I was speaking about social media. She said she found it hard to find the time to keep up with her social media accounts. I understand that this can be challenging, so I recommended: 'To start with, allocate 10 minutes in the morning, 10 minutes at lunchtime and 10 minutes at the end of the day. If even that's too much, just do it twice a day.'

'I know, I know, that's what everyone tells me. But I've got a young daughter,' she said, as if that explained it all. I wanted to point out that there are 200 million Twitter users in the world and 900 million Facebook users. And I'm pretty sure that a fair chunk of them have daughters. Hell, some have two. Some even have sons, who I suspect could be even more time-consuming.

'Can you afford to outsource it?' I asked.

'Oh no, I've only just started my business. We're not even making money.'

'Well … if you don't do it … *who else is going to*?'

For those who say they're too busy, I know it can be hard to find the time to share your stories on social media. But that's tantamount to saying that you don't have time to do the accounting, you don't have time to do any marketing or you don't have time to serve customers. It's a key operation in your business that simply can't be ignored.

So who will actually share your stories on social media? Your choices are: you, a team member or an agency.

You

If you're bootstrapping and don't have staff or budget, then you're it, baby. Don't think you need to study every single media platform on the planet before you jump in. Just sign up—it's almost always free—and start lurking. Watch what everyone else is doing for a couple of weeks before you get active.

Which ones should you sign up for? The big three are Twitter, Facebook and LinkedIn. At the very least, sign up for these. Of course, there are many others, but don't feel the need to open an account with every one if you're just getting started. It's better first to focus on the ones you know currently get the most traffic and explore the others later.

A team member

If you have a team member who understands social media, you might want to give this responsibility to them. Don't underestimate the importance of it by giving it to the intern or transient backpacker. You need a professional who understands your brand, is committed to customer service and, ideally, can also spell!

An agency

There are pros and cons to outsourcing to an agency. At the heart of this debate is the issue of authenticity. After all, if your business is tweeting and facebooking, some people would argue that it should be you (or someone from your team) doing this, not another organisation. As the volume of social media interactions increases, however, the number of businesses that outsource to agencies is doing the same.

If you go down this route, then the key is to ensure the agency you choose has a clear understanding of:

- your brand and the products you offer
- how to deal with any customer service issues (who should they pass these on to within your organisation?)
- who owns the social media data such as details of followers, demographic information and metrics. (Hint: that would be you!)

'I'm a private person. I don't want to share my life online'

The key thing to remember here is that you are in control. You decide what you want to share online and what you don't. If you don't want to share it, don't.

Too often, I come across business owners who have not made a foray into social media because they think it's an invasion of their privacy. Or they think that in order to succeed and develop a following, they need to bare their souls, let their skeletons out of the closet and tweet about every event in their lives. I recently ran a blogging workshop for a group of people keen to build their online profile. Their concerns had a recurring theme:

• 'I don't want to post photos of my kids.' *Then don't.*
• 'I don't want to blog about my divorce.' *That's okay, keep it to yourself.*
• 'Why do I have to put it all out there?' *Who said you had to do that?*

There's no rule in the social media guidebook that says you need to bare all. You just need to be authentic. While some people choose to live their lives online and feel totally at ease with sharing intimate details about their sex life, mental state and fractured relationships, that doesn't mean you have to be one of them.

There's a difference between revealing details about what should remain 'personal' and revealing details about your 'personality'. It's fine for the former to remain off limits, but it's vital to reveal the latter.

Let's say you're a recruitment consultant. If you only share white papers about salary packaging or tweet about jobs you're trying to fill, you'll have only a limited base of followers. Chances are they will be your competitors and they're just following you to keep tabs on what you're doing. Like building any kind of relationship in real life, people need to get to know you before they begin to like and trust you, and that means they need to find a way to connect with you as a person.

Living in a public space

Julien Smith first made his name as a commentator and futurist on technology and social media, co-writing the best-selling book *Trust Agents* with Chris Brogan. The first thing that strikes you about him is his voice, so it's no surprise to find that Julien has been a professional voice actor and radio broadcaster. He talks a mile a minute with an intensity that is strangely mesmerising. I think I could listen to him read the phonebook.

With the web becoming an increasingly crowded marketplace, Julien has focused much of his work on how to stand out and build a profile while also doing what you need to become a better person. This unique perspective has gained him a near cult following.

I first meet Julien, who is based in Montreal, three months after the publication of *The Flinch*, his manifesto-style book about transforming yourself to become more physically and psychologically resistant. The book had already been downloaded 100 000 times (it was released, only as an ebook, as part of Seth Godin's innovative publishing venture The Domino Project <www.thedominoproject. com>). By the time you read this, that number will be even bigger. Probably much bigger.

While I'm chatting to Julien, our conversation is interrupted by the squeals of a woman, in her forties, sitting opposite us. She's realised who he is, and she's clearly a follower of the cult of Julien.

'You're the reason I scream every morning,' she said excitedly.

I raise an eyebrow. Even mile-a-minute Julien seems at a loss for words.

'When I take a shower,' she says by way of explanation.

In *The Flinch*, Julien sets readers 'homework assignments' to help them get over resistance to change and to let go of fear. One is to take a cold shower—a really cold shower—every day for a week.

The woman (we'll call her Margie) had discovered Julien online. She'd never seen him speak in real life, she had never met him until that moment, but she had read his books and blog religiously. Margie followed Julien's unconventional advice because she trusted him. And that trust could be built because Julien put his ideas, experience and life online. But when you read Julien's blog <www.inoveryourhead.net> or google him, you're not going to find deep dark personal secrets; he doesn't post countless photos of his family and friends. He lets you into *part* of his life.

'You need to expose yourself,' says Julien. 'The more hidden you are, the harder it is for people to get to know or like you. But the more visible you are, the easier it becomes for people to relate to the work that you do. I would say that the best life in the modern world is lived in a public space where you have the ability to connect with people in a very simple way. You make obvious what you care about, and then have the ability to capture and follow up on conversations about that — through either your blog or whatever platform you decide to use.'

If you're still resisting the idea of sharing your stories online — or *flinching*, as Julien would put it — think of it this way. Imagine resisting the benefits of air travel. Sure, you can shun the idea of ever getting on a plane. And there are always alternative options to get you from A to B — car, ship, horse and carriage … But if you do resist, it's going to take you a hell of a lot longer to get to your destination. And, once you do, your competition will have already established a presence in the market. They may even dominate it.

Like anything in the world, the way we do business needs to evolve, particularly in relation to the social web. Julien compares it to being in a forge or furnace where metals are refined to create tools. 'A business needs to evolve in order to withstand new kinds of pressure,' he says. 'That's why I call it a forge. It is the pressure of the new business environment, and any company that is not able to withstand that kind of pressure is fundamentally fragile. The way you deal with it shows what you are made of, and your business will either be transformed or destroyed in the process.

'It needs to become a different kind of animal than the animal it used to be in order to survive. There was a reason massive woolly mammoths evolved into smaller elephants with all these different features. The environment changed so the animal had to evolve. Every species has had to change over time in order to adapt to a new environment, or it would die off. A business has to do the same thing, and so do individuals if they're trying to develop a personal brand.'

Like it or not, you're in that forge. And the way business is done these days, the way connections are made and stories are shared, is totally different compared with a mere five years ago. So you have a choice. You can stick with what you've always done and get left behind. Or you can adapt to the new world.

Your actions

Story sharing

Imagine knowing that there is a dinner party going on that you're not invited to. People are talking about you, but you have no idea what they're saying. The first step in your strategy is to join the dinner party so you can take part in the conversation. The next step is to host the dinner party. Here's how:

1 If you haven't already signed up to at least Twitter, Facebook and LinkedIn, do it now. You can add other social platforms later.
2 Lurk and learn. Just watch the interactions around you and observe what people talk about.
3 If you're new to social media, pick one platform to focus on. If you spread yourself too thinly, you won't mine the real value of any of them.
4 Don't be afraid to experiment, as long as you stay polite, respectful and generous with sharing your advice and information.
5 Share your stories through links to your blog posts, links to other people's posts, uploading YouTube videos, connecting with customers, and so on. And remember to inject personality into your updates.

CHAPTER 11

What's your story?

As Louise sat at her computer she was a mouse click away from changing her life forever. At home in her small country town in Quebec, Canada, she had two young kids and was trying to make ends meet. Just two words. Staring at the screen, she had no idea that those two words would have such an impact. But there they were blinking back at her:

James Chartrand

That was the day Louise chose to use a pen name — and her life has never been the same.

It was 2006 and Louise was relatively new to the world of freelance writing. Living in a town heavily reliant on summer tourist traffic, when winter came she found herself without an income. 'I didn't have any job prospects in sight,' she says, 'and money was running out.' Drawing on her hobby of fiction writing, she began finding small writing jobs online, some paying only $2 per article. Not per word, *per article*. This work was mainly for content mills.

If you're not familiar with the way content mills (or content farms) work, they typically use large numbers of low-paid freelancers to generate articles on various topics. These are used to populate sites that are designed simply to draw as many visitors as possible so it can earn money from advertising. Typically, the expectation of quality is nowhere near as high as a mainstream news site featuring writing by journalists. Even today it's not uncommon to find content mills paying as little as $1 to $10 per article.

'There isn't a lot of respect between writers at that level,' she says. 'There aren't a lot of men doing that sort of writing at that level either. It's a very female-dominated industry, because it's flexible hours and you can work from home, so that makes it very easy for women with children. I had no experience whatsoever, and when you're new to this you don't know any better. You just think, "Wow, someone is going to pay me to write." So you write articles on anything from yeast infections to dollhouses to how to make peanut butter.'

Quite simply, Louise did what she had to in order to support her family. And with few other options, she persisted. Trying to get ahead, Louise attempted to expand her small writing business by hiring other freelance writers like her. She placed an advertisement online—and that's when she noticed something.

'I quickly found out that when you're a woman and you're dealing with other writers who are women at that level in the industry, where the pay is low, it's very catty. It's very competitive and people are quite nasty. They don't necessarily have the business skills and experience to conduct a professional relationship.

'I also noticed that most of the people who were hiring me were men.' So she decided to conduct an experiment. She gave herself a randomly chosen pen name, James Chartrand. That's when everything changed.

Until then she had placed advertisements looking for freelance writers under her own name. This time she used her pen name. 'The difference in the response was substantial. Very substantial. The people who applied to me as James were much more respectful than the people who applied to Louise.'

For a few months she had two websites, one for Louise and one for James. She began applying for writing jobs as Louise and then applying for the same job as James.

'By then I was specialising in copywriting for websites, which paid a lot more than the content mills,' she says. 'The clients were willing to pay much higher rates to James. When a client thought I was female, they would haggle, they wanted to bargain with me and they made it clear that I was a woman working from home with kids hanging off my legs. When I applied for jobs under my pen name James Chartrand, the difference was phenomenal.

'People really admired that James worked from home and there was a much higher level of respect. Clients wouldn't try to negotiate on my price and they listened to my feedback and acted on it. Whereas when I presented ideas as a woman, they would often question my opinion or thank me politely but ignore my suggestions.'

Using only email to communicate with clients, James never had to reveal the fact he was a she. It wasn't long before Louise decided to stop writing under her real name. She let that website go and simply continued on as James. 'I just decided that it wasn't worth it to keep the female perception going,' she says. 'At that point I had a single goal, which was to earn an income, to feed my kids and get ahead. I wanted a life where I was treated like a person, where nobody questioned my rates or tried to bargain me down.'

As James Chartrand she began blogging about writing and shot to prominence when her blog won a place on the 'Top 10 Blogs for Writers' compiled by Michael Stelzner in 2007. 'I got a lot of traffic from it,' she says. 'I didn't expect to be popular. I didn't expect to be noticed. Then I was kind of stuck, because at that point you can't turn around and say, "Actually, that's not me." At the same time I thought, "This is working so why shouldn't I keep it going?"'

From there, James began to market herself online, contributing to other high-profile blogs including Brian Clark's popular *Copyblogger*. Today her own blog, <www.menwithpens.ca>, has more than 40 000 readers, a number that continues to grow. By 2008 she didn't need to look for work anymore — it was walking in the door. 'Since 2009, demand has been far more than I can support,' she says.

Once a struggling single mother trying to make a modest income to raise her two kids, Louise changed her life by changing her story.

Or rather, she changed the name of the main character, and the raft of assumptions that went with it.

It's not an original approach. Female writers all over the world have done this for various reasons. Miles Franklin, author of the Australian classic *My Brilliant Career*, was Stella Franklin. Even *Harry Potter* author J.K. Rowling, whose real name is Joanne, was asked by her publishers to use her initials because they feared that the target readership of young boys wouldn't want to read a book by a woman.

James Chartrand's business boomed. Her path followed a true Entrepreneur's Journey, because, as we've learned, even after you win the prize there are more ordeals lurking around the corner. 'It was very stressful because in the back of my mind I was always thinking: what if this all blows up?' she says. Each time clients asked to speak with her on the phone, she found excuses to keep the relationship strictly over email. 'I'd tell them it's better to have a written record of our work.'

But challenges also came from unexpected quarters. Although James never appeared in a photo online, 'he' garnered his share of romantic attention. Readers flirted with James over email and some took it a step further. One particular client had become a friend. 'We would email back and forth. At one point she revealed that she was actually having feelings about me. I said, "Well, you know what? We had better get on the phone and talk about this." When she found out I was a woman she was just crushed.

'She was angry for some time, but she emailed me later on to say that though she was still very upset about what happened, the fact that she had been having those thoughts and dreaming them actually showed her she did have a big problem in her relationship. She has since left her husband, taken her two kids and started over. She thanked me for shaking up her world in that way.'

However, everything came to a head for James. Just as James was riding a wave of success, someone threatened to bring it all down. 'I had a friend who had worked with me for several years doing some web design work. In 2009 we had a falling out. She was a little bit bitter and I understand that. It's an emotional situation when things aren't working out. And she began telling people.

'My first reaction was to get in touch with her and say, "Please stop." But she had decided she was not going to stop. So I decided these are my actions, my consequences to live with, and I'm not going to sit by and let someone else control what happens to me in my life. This was *my* story to tell.'

'I decided that I wanted to grab the biggest microphone I could find and blow it up out of the water. I'd make an absolute clean break and explosion and get it out there and done with.' James outed herself on Brian Clark's *Copyblogger* blog under a post called 'James Chartrand wears women's underpants'.

The news spread like wildfire online and James fielded interviews from radio and TV for three weeks. She also attracted attacks from feminists who doubted her story or felt it was done as a publicity stunt. Others felt betrayed. There were also those who ripped her apart, saying she should have fought harder as a woman instead of playing the game under a male name.

But James never sought to be a lobbyist or champion for women writers. And most people, she says, were supportive, many of them understanding the gender bias she faced, often because they were facing it themselves. 'It wasn't worth fighting over, complaining over, getting angry about. It wasn't an emotional or a personal thing, it was just business. I'm here to support my family. One way worked, the other didn't.'

James is quick to point out that she did not create a persona. 'Creating a persona means you are imagining a person with a personality that you do not have, like an actor,' she says. 'I never adopted a persona, because I was always myself. It was just a name and the gender association that I led people to believe that was different. The persona was never different from who I was.'

Since being outed, James makes it clear that 'James Chartrand' is her pen name, featuring her (real and female) photo on her site. Business has continued to boom. She runs a successful website copywriting and design business and teaches a writing course designed specifically for business owners. (For more, see the exclusive resources section at <www.powerstoriesbook.com>.)

Ultimately, James chose to live the story that worked for her. As author of her story she chose to be a successful copywriter who gained a worldwide following and happens to use a male name, rather than a struggling single mother barely eking out a living.

What's your story?

This is the eighth and final power story you should have in your arsenal—the story that drives your life.

I don't mean your memoir or autobiography. This isn't a line you'll use in an elevator or feature on your website. In fact, it is a story you may never even tell anyone. And yet it's probably the most important story of them all.

You are the main character in your own story. Have you cast yourself as the hero, the leader, the rock star? Are you the exhausted mother, the victim, or the writer finding success working under a pen name? Or are you the guy who's just trying to support his family even if it means he hates going to work? Like James, you're the author of your own story. So if you're not happy with the way you've been cast, it's up to you to rewrite it.

You might think that's easier said than done. After all, if you're the guy supporting his family, your kids and mortgage aren't about to disappear any time soon. You're stuck in a work situation you don't like but this is the hand you've been dealt, you think, and there's no point trying to dress it up to look like anything else.

If you're a business owner, are you building a powerful business despite the difficult economic climate? Or are you hard done by because the government has slugged you with high tax and your sneaky competitors have undercut your pricing?

The reality is that the words you choose to use—even in the story that's simply going on in your head—can have a power beyond measure. The narrative you tell yourself about why your life is the way it is will have a profound impact on your actions, happiness and success.

When you're in business, it can be so easy to get caught up in the daily grind of life. There are problems to solve, customers to service, fires to put out, tax to pay and everything in between. It's a treadmill that doesn't stop. But if you force yourself to stop and look at the life you're living, ask yourself: *Is this the story I expected to be telling about my life? Is this what I really wanted?*

For some people, the answer is a resounding 'Yes!' Others will shake their head and wonder how they ended up living a life that isn't at all what they expected, when deep down they'd wanted something extraordinary. This moment of reflection, which can literally last a moment or can take weeks or months, often brings a profound realisation that they've let someone else — or something else — write their story. They've lived up to the expectations of their parents, they've been buffeted along to fit in with the changing needs of their family. Or they've been held back by the inertia of their unambitious friends. They might even be in a rut and, thanks to this inertia, their story hasn't changed in years. It's been stuck on the same page.

At the Sydney Writers' Centre, one of our most popular courses is Life Writing. An integral part of the course is to write about the reality of your life — to write your life story in all its glory, pain, colour and darkness. Often this is the first time people have taken the time to examine the story they have been living, and many are taken aback to realise that they have been living other people's expectations of their lives. The good news is that many also then realise they can take back the authorship of their own lives. They understand that they can control the narrative. They need to live their own story.

What story do you want to live? And what do you need to change to make that happen? When you figure this out, you can't just dream of this happening some day. It's going to happen only if you believe the story to be true and if you start taking small steps to turn it into reality. Remember, you are the author. It's your choice if you want to cast yourself as the hero, the success or the failure, or the victim. If you want to change your life, you need to change your story.

Stories for entrepreneurs

Peter Shallard is a psychiatrist based in New York City whose clients are busy entrepreneurs. That sounds like the opening voiceover of a Woody Allen movie. However, when I talk with Peter in the Meatpacking District in Chelsea, there are no neurotic intellectuals pacing the pavements nearby. In fact, although Peter is now firmly entrenched in New York life, this New Zealand–born therapist previously ran his practice from Sydney.

These days his client roster is more global than ever. His clients range from those building multimillion-dollar empires with thousands of staff to business owners with only a handful of employees. And Peter has turned the tradition of the therapy session on the shrink's couch on its head. Thanks to the convenience of phone, email and time zone converters, he consults to clients around the world.

Peter first worked in clinical therapy helping people with issues such as anxiety, depression and addictions, but since 2006 he has specialised in working with business clients and describes himself as 'The Shrink for Entrepreneurs'.

Peter also believes that entrepreneurs should choose the right stories. In the same way that the right music can pump up athletes before they compete, the right stories can also inspire, teach and motivate.

'If you're in a leadership position where you're running a team of 1000 people, you might want to look at military narratives about great generals. You'd find tactical stories about leaders who inspired loyalty and motivated armies to follow them into battle,' says Peter. 'Our unconscious minds respond to metaphorical learning and latch on to concepts in a way that we can never process consciously.

'It's the same as the idea that the quality of a novelist is really determined by the quality of their library. The quality of an entrepreneur is determined by the quality of their experience, and that includes what they've learned about the experiences of other business people. That's why we like to read business books and biographies of successful entrepreneurs.

'It's not just through books. It's also about the entrepreneur who catches up with their tycoon uncle for lunch once a week and listens to his business stories. That person is going to have this richness and depth to their intelligence around how to make decisions, how to communicate, how to succeed as an entrepreneur.'

Peter suggests it's also worthwhile emulating and sharing stories of the person you'd like to be. The version that's the next step up from who you are right now. 'Convey the version of you that you want to be,' says Peter, 'because before long, you will become that version. Everybody is aware of the room they have for improvement in their lives. We all tell ourselves these stories about who we'd like to become.'

If you share your life online to build your personal brand, it's vital to be strategic about it. Welcome to the world of personality marketing. Some entrepreneurs shun the limelight, hate Facebook, don't understand blogs and can't understand why so many people whip out their smartphones to 'check in' or take photos of their food as soon as it arrives. If that's you, move along. This part's not for you. Read chapter 10 and then come back here.

If you want to build your personal brand online, remember that you can edit the story you decide to share online. Whether it's a well-crafted tweet, a strategically chosen photo or a Foursquare 'check in' at a hip venue, you can edit out the mundane and present the shiny version of your life.

You're not inventing a fictional new character. You just need to be yourself. Or rather, the shiny, improved version of yourself. In other words, determine what your personal brand is all about—what you want other people to be saying about you when you're not there. If you want to be a successful business mentor who travels the world, is location independent and goes to cool events, then they are the stories you should be sharing.

You might share:

- photos on Facebook of you speaking at a high-profile seminar
- a blog post about how you can continue running your business even though you are poolside in the Maldives
- tweets from the wifi-enabled cabin on a Virgin flight from New York to Los Angeles.

You wouldn't share:

- the bulk buy bargain cereal you found at Costco
- how you waited at home for the plumber to fix whatever was stuck in the S-bend
- a tweet about how cranky you are to be stuck in traffic.

Those last three examples may be true, but should you be sharing them as part of your story? I know it's important to be authentic, but remember that as the author of your own story, you get to edit.

No author spews out *everything* that's in their brain to let the world pick through it for points of interest. Well, no good author anyway. Every good story goes through an editing process. This is where messages are refined, sentences are tweaked and plot lines are shaped so it's easier for the reader to digest. That's what you need to do with your story.

Peter has experienced it in his own life. An avid online connector, Peter has a popular blog at <www.petershallard.com> and is active on social media. 'When I started blogging in 2009, I realised it's very public. What you put online is for everyone to see. I don't blog about my client work because that's completely private. But I do blog about myself. And I started blogging about the parts of myself where I'm confident and successful. I started developing this narrative about the next version of myself.' Put simply, the person Peter is today is probably the version of him he blogged about six months ago.

'Not only do you believe that you can be that next version, but when you get a following of people who are invested in your narrative—who like to follow what you do—it inspires you to go out and do bigger and better things. The fact that you know other people are following your story motivates you to do more, to become more.'

Even if you don't want to tell stories about your life, Peter points out that you are already doing so. 'We're all telling narratives all the time. We're on Facebook posting status updates. And if we're not on Facebook, we're telling them to our kids and our partners. When you're asked: "What did you do at work today, honey?", the answer to that is a chunk of narrative. The only difference between a person who's having a conversation with their spouse at the end of the day and somebody who's telling their stories on a blog or other medium is the audience and the platform. You can choose the story you want to tell.'

For those who question the legitimacy of telling the story of the next version of yourself, Peter simply says: 'To ask whether that's not authentic is basically to ask if it is inauthentic to have aspirations. Plus when you tell stories of aspiration—stories about the goals you have and about what you want to achieve—you know that people are following your story. And, for most people, especially entrepreneurs, that motivates you further.'

If you don't actively shape your story and the character you want to be, then other people will do it based on the fragments of information or gossip or hearsay they find out about you. Depending on where they get their information—the media, the school gates, random tweets and so on—they will create their own perception of you, whether or not it's true.

So unless you actively create your story as the hero, or the successful entrepreneur, or the loving parent, or the location-independent business owner, then they will cast you in the role they see. That could be anything from the overworked business owner to the nice-but-not-too-smart soccer mum or a class-A bitch. Why let other people create their version of you when *your* version of you is so much better?

We've already seen that the power stories we tell others can persuade people to buy, move them to action or inspire them to change the world. The right stories can also build your profile and grow your business. But without a doubt the most important power story of them all is the one you tell yourself. It's your compass, the framework on which you can base your decisions—and a path to your future.

You are the author and you are in complete control of what is about to unfold. Whatever challenges come your way, you can determine how to overcome them. You can be the hero, or you can be the victim. You alone can shape the next powerful chapter in your journey.

Your actions

Your story

This power story is going to shape the rest of your life. So take the time to craft it now. But remember that it's not set in stone. You can edit, restructure the chapters and even change the characters if that's what you want, because you are the author. But you have to get started or your story will collect dust, and it won't be a life that's lived.

Follow the steps below or download Your Story template in the exclusive resources section at <www.powerstoriesbook.com>.

1 Imagine the 'new and improved' version of you. That's the 'you' where you're confident, happy and successful. For some, that's going to be reflected in the amount of money you make. For others, it's going to be about being confident in your appearance and presentation. Yet others

will measure this by relationships and high-level networking opportunities. The point is that everyone is different: determine what works for you.

2 Write down what this looks like. For example, if you want a higher level of networking and are keen to mix with more successful peers, write down who you'd like to see in your circle. If you want to be more confident in your presentation, write down how you actually see yourself. Aim to identify 10 different points, and be as specific as you can in describing this next version of you.

3 Pick any three of these points. Act as if you are already living your story. Some will be easy. Others will take a few steps before you get there, but determine what those steps are and then take them.

4 If you're comfortable doing so, share your story with other people. You don't have to do this but, if you do, it can help you stay accountable and motivate you to action.

Conclusion
So what's next?

Now we've reached the end of our story together. You know the eight power stories you must tell to build an epic business. So don't just read this book and leave it on your shelf. Now it's time to put these ideas into action.

This book offers a blueprint that will help you grow your business, build your profile and get ahead of the pack. Download the templates, follow the instructions, emulate the examples. Connect the dots with stories from your own life and business.

If you're still wondering whether these power stories will really help to grow your business, well, there's only one way to find out. You can use them and discover how effective they are. Or you can ignore them and keep doing what you've always been doing. These power stories are so effective because when you craft them in the right way they are easy to remember and to share. And that's where you start getting leverage from them—when other people do your storytelling for you.

I know you're a busy entrepreneur. But creating these eight power stories won't take as long as you think, because most of them already exist. They're part of your wealth of experience, already embedded in your psyche. In many cases, they've been told before.

But in order to use them effectively, you need to take the time to identify and articulate them. You don't want to just string some sentences together and hope you've conveyed your message. You want beautifully crafted and packaged stories. You want stories people will relate to, stories they are going to share, stories that build your business, convert sales and nurture a legion of raving fans.

Remember, if you want to build an epic business, you need an epic story. And that starts right here.

What's your story?

Join our community at <www.powerstoriesbook.com>.

Acknowledgements

This book would not have been possible without the support of my team at the Sydney Writers' Centre in Milsons Point, especially Danielle Williams, Tracy Tan, Rose Powell and Andrew Gillman. Thanks to everyone at Wiley: especially Lucy Raymond, for embracing this project, and Jem Bates for his skilful editing. Also to Laura Callow for demonstrating that it's possible to get a book deal via Twitter. Thanks to the Kimono crew (you know who you are) for your feedback and to my wonderful friends who put up with me when I went into hibernation to write this book. Huge appreciation also to all the entrepreneurs in this book for trusting me to tell your stories.

VALERIE
KHOO

The perils and pleasures of running your own small business. The excitement of big ideas in the wee small hours. Welcome to Valerie Khoo's blog – covering her passions for writing, technology, productivity and entrepreneurship.

Exploring real-time issues in a real-world way, you'll discover something new every visit – practical, topical and thought provoking.

You'll find her insights and resources as a business founder, investor, and mentor to businesses and startups.

There are even freebies. Visit Valerie's blog to receive her free report on *Storytelling Secrets of Highly Profitable Businesses*, including a guide on how to build your profile using Twitter, Facebook and by creating podcasts.

www.ValerieKhoo.com
Inspiration, innovation and insights.